EASY PIANO

IRVING BERLIN'S

God Bless America®

& Other American Inspirations

W9-ARO-609

ABOUT "GOD BLESS AMERICA"

"GOD BLESS AMERICA" by Irving Berlin was first published in 1938. Almost as soon as the song began generating revenue, Mr. Berlin established The God Bless America Fund to benefit American youth.

Over $6,000,000 has been distributed to date, primarily to two youth organizations with which Mr. and Mrs. Berlin were personally involved: the Girl Scout Council of Greater New York, and the Greater New York Councils of the Boy Scouts of America. These councils do not discriminate on any basis and are committed to serving all segments of New York City's diverse youth population.

The trustees of The God Bless America Fund are working with the two councils to ensure that funding is allocated for New York City children affected by the tragic events of September 11, 2001.

ISBN 0-634-04006-5

GOD BLESS AMERICA is a registered trademark of the
Trustees of the God Bless America Fund

HAL•LEONARD®
CORPORATION

7777 W. BLUEMOUND RD. P.O. BOX 13819 MILWAUKEE, WI 53213

Visit Hal Leonard Online at
www.halleonard.com

Contents

ABRAHAM, MARTIN AND JOHN

Words and Music by
RICHARD HOLLER

Moderate Rock beat

Pedal optional

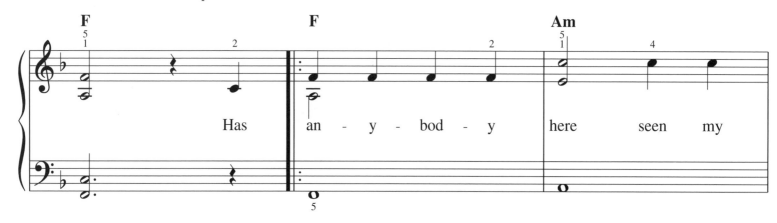

Has an - y - bod - y here seen my

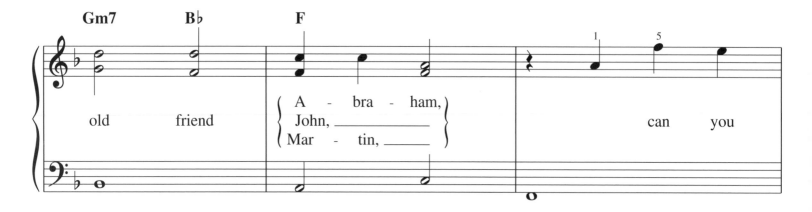

old friend { A - bra - ham, / John, _____ / Mar - tin, _____ } can you

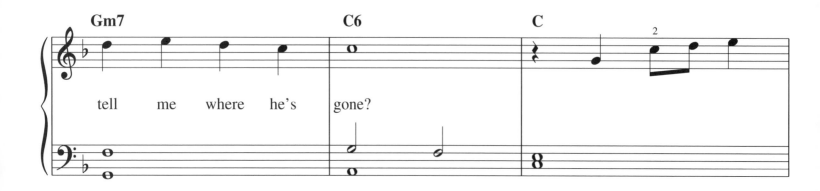

tell me where he's gone?

5

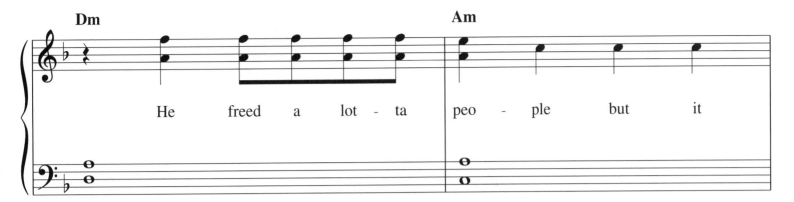

He freed a lotta peo - ple but it

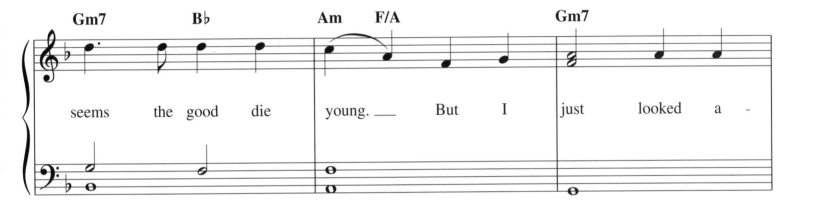

seems the good die young. ___ But I just looked a -

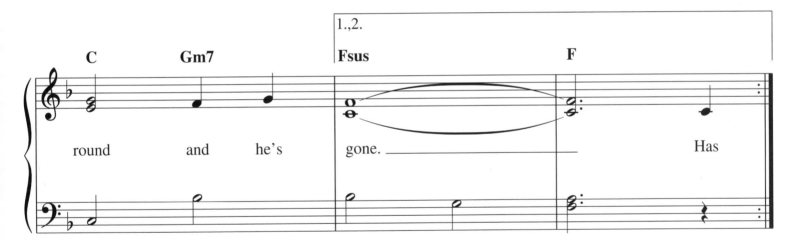

round and he's gone. ___ Has

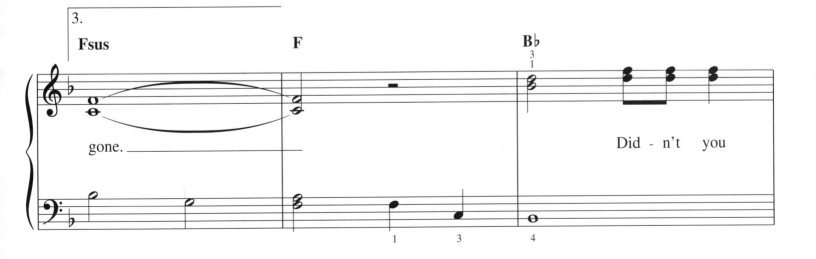

gone. ___ Did - n't you

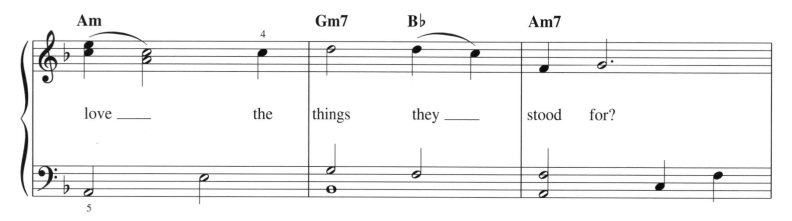

love _____ the things they _____ stood for?

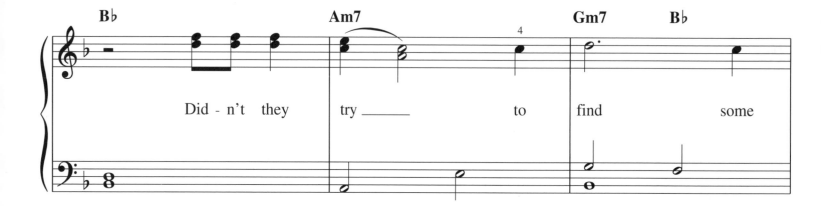

Did - n't they try _____ to find some

good for you and me? And

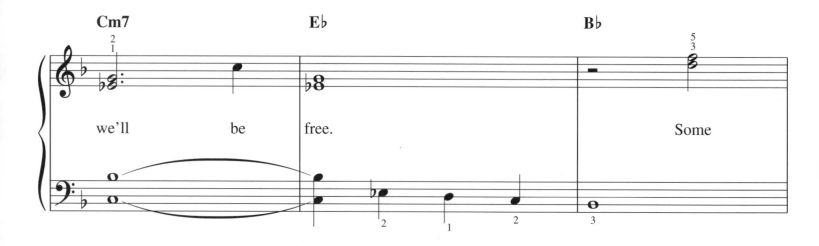

we'll be free. Some

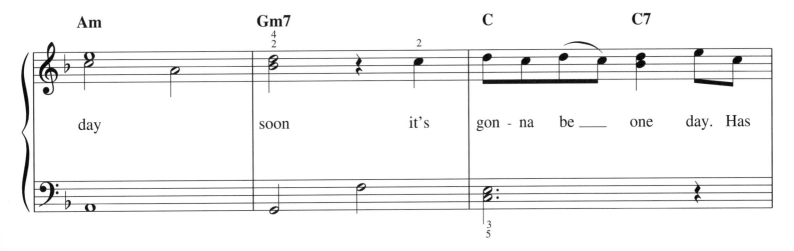

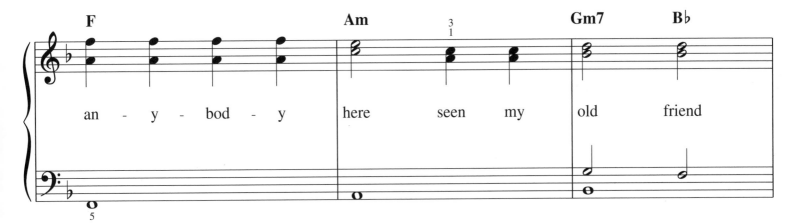

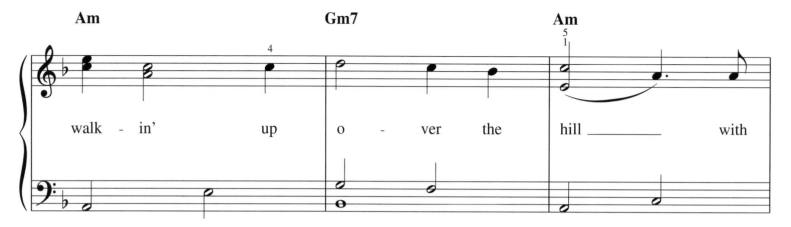

walk - in'   up   o - ver the   hill _____ with

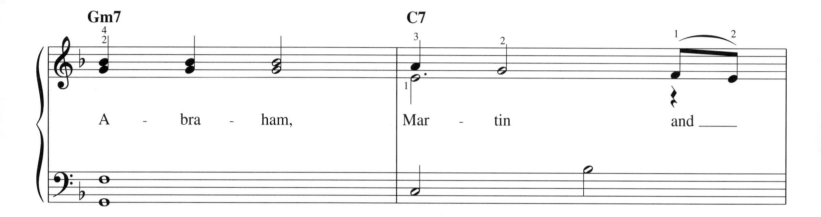

A - bra - ham,   Mar - tin   and ____

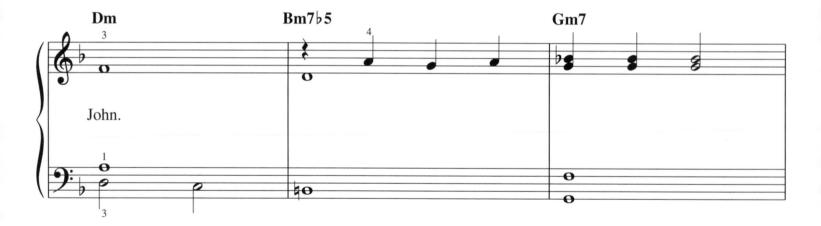

John.

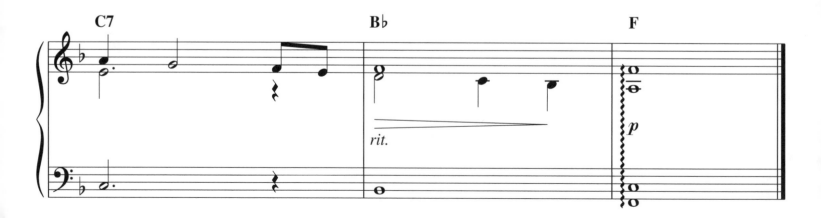

rit.

AMAZING GRACE

Words by JOHN NEWTON
Traditional American Melody

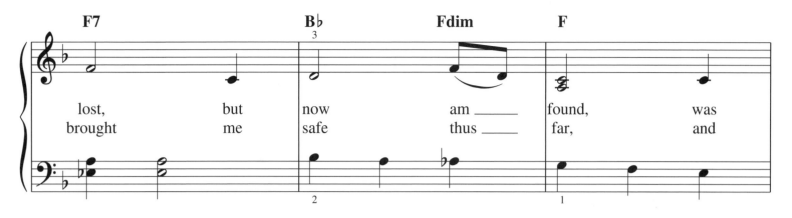

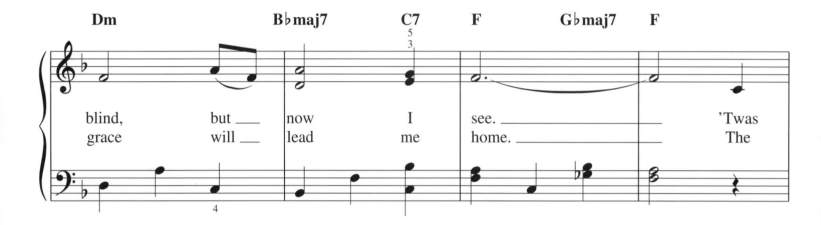

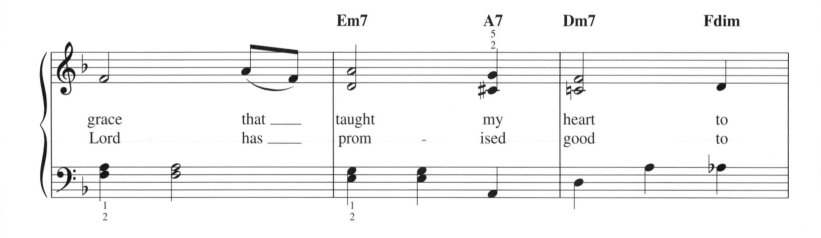

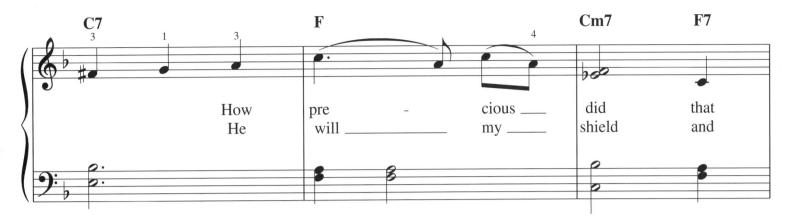

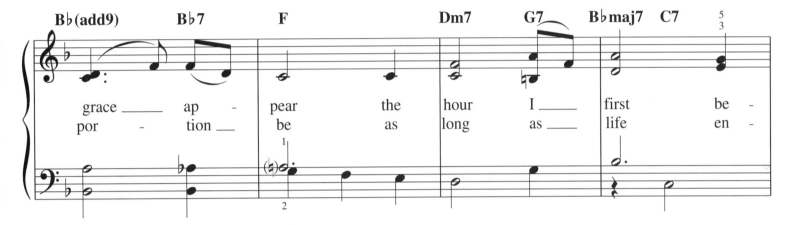

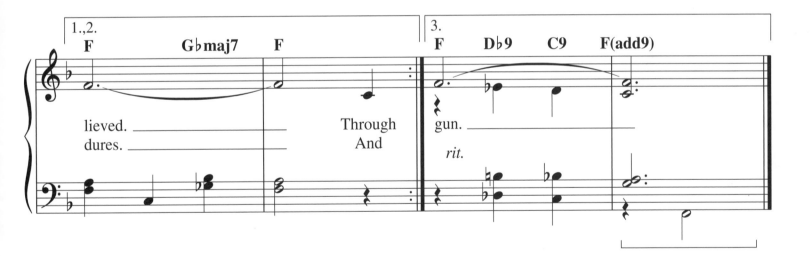

Additional Lyrics

3. And when this flesh and heart shall fail
And mortal life shall cease.
I shall possess within the veil
A life of joy and peace.
When we've been there ten thousand years,
Bright shining as the sun
We've no less days to sing God's praise
Than when we first begun.

AMERICA, THE BEAUTIFUL

Words by KATHERINE LEE BATES
Music by SAMUEL A. WARD

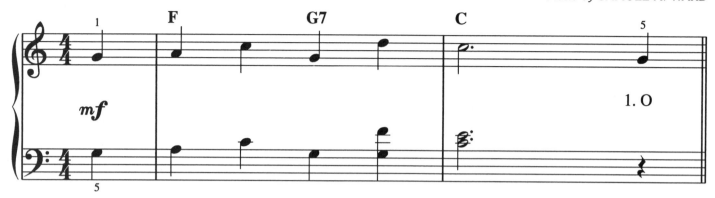

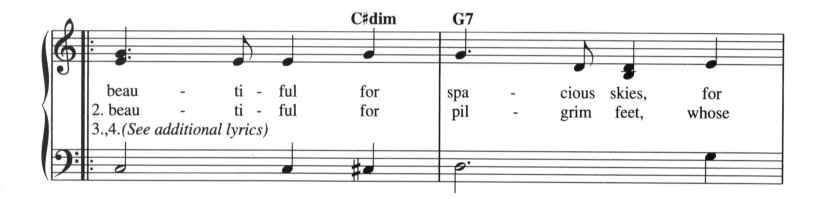

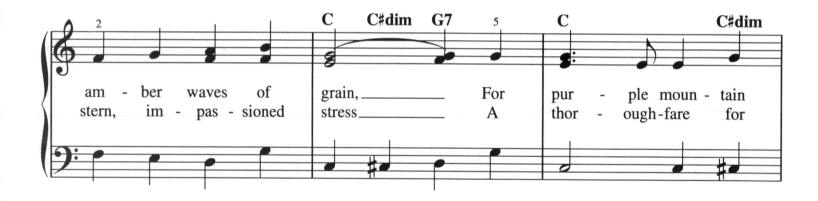

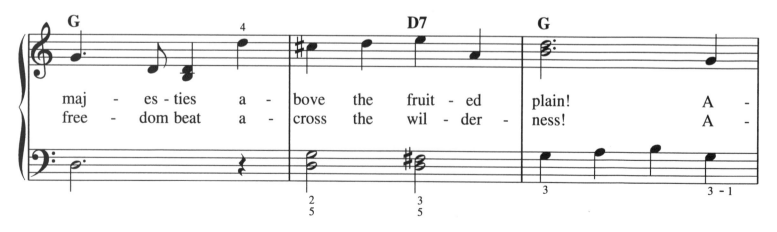

13

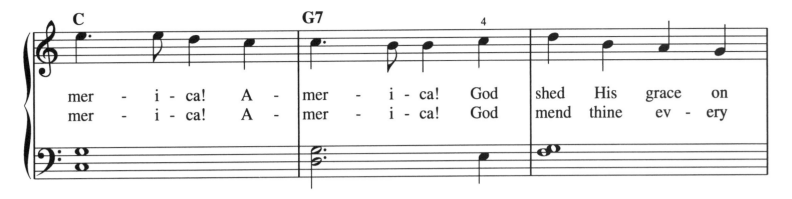

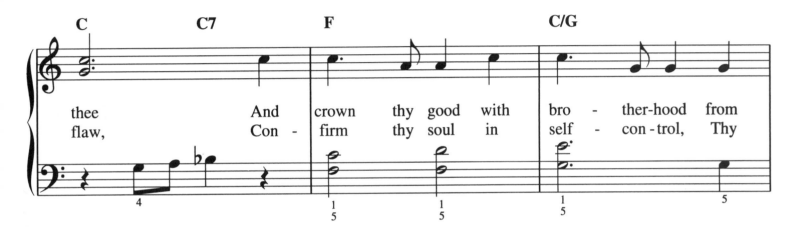

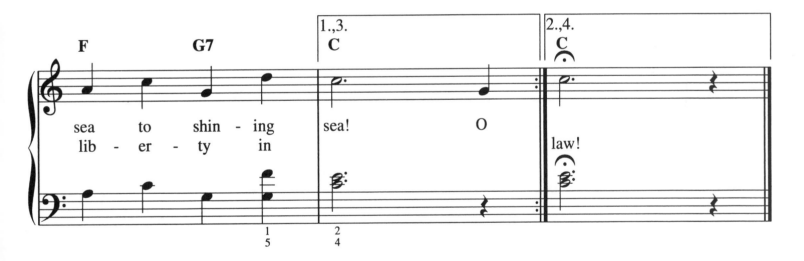

Additional Lyrics

3. O beautiful for heroes proved in liberating strife,
   Who more than self their country loved, and mercy more than life!
   America! America! May God thy gold refine,
   Till all success be nobleness and every gain divine!

4. O beautiful for patriot dream that sees beyond the years
   Thine alabaster cities gleam undimmed by human tears!
   America! America! God shed His grace on thee,
   And crown thy good with brotherhood from sea to shining sea!

BATTLE HYMN OF THE REPUBLIC

Words by JULIA WARD HOWE
Music by WILLIAM STEFFE

Moderate march tempo

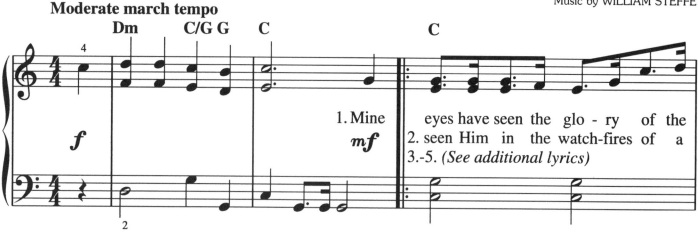

1. Mine eyes have seen the glo - ry of the
2. seen Him in the watch-fires of a
3.-5. *(See additional lyrics)*

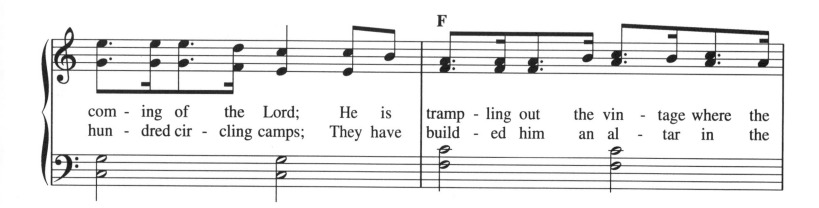

com - ing of the Lord; He is tramp - ling out the vin - tage where the
hun - dred cir - cling camps; They have build - ed him an al - tar in the

grapes of wrath are stored; He hath loos'd the fate - ful light - ning of His
eve - ning dews and damps; I have read his right - eous sen - tence by the

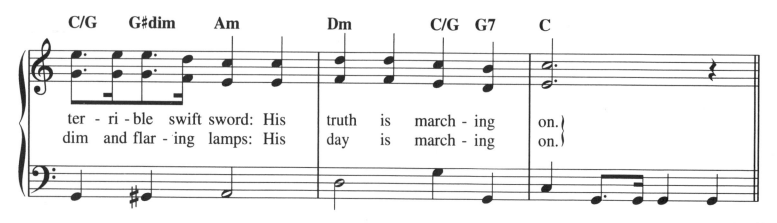

ter - ri - ble swift sword: His truth is march - ing on.}
dim and flar - ing lamps: His day is march - ing on.}

Chorus

Glo - ry, glo - ry, hal - le - lu - jah! Glo - ry, glo - ry, hal - le -

lu - jah! Glo - ry, glo - ry, hal - le - lu - jah! His

truth is march - ing on. I have on.

Additional Lyrics

3. I have read a fiery gospel writ in burnished rows of steel:
   "As ye deal with my condemners, so with you my grace shall deal;
   Let the Hero, born of woman, crush the serpent with his heel,
   Since God is marching on."
   To Chorus:

4. He has sounded forth the trumpet that shall never call retreat;
   He is sifting out the hearts of men before His judgement seat:
   Oh, be swift, my soul, to answer Him! be jubilant, my feet!
   Our God is marching on.
   To Chorus:

5. In the beauty of the lilies, Christ was born across the sea,
   With a glory in His bosom that transfigures you and me:
   As He died to make men holy, let us die to make men free,
   While God is marching on.
   To Chorus:

COUNT YOUR BLESSINGS
INSTEAD OF SHEEP

from the Motion Picture Irving Berlin's WHITE CHRISTMAS

Words and Music by
IRVING BERLIN

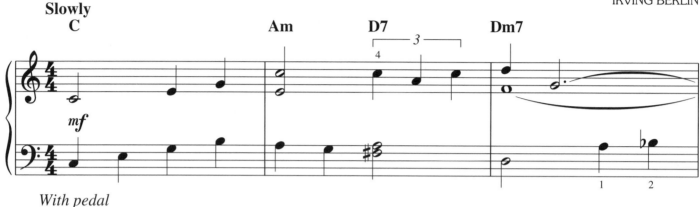

With pedal

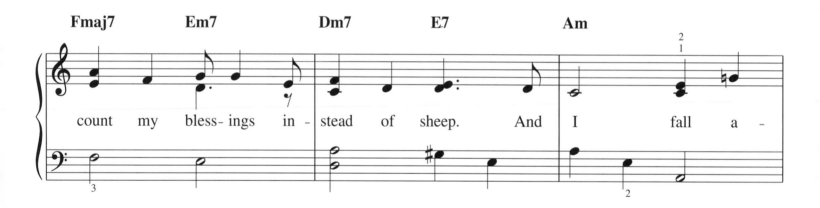

When I'm wor-ried and I can't sleep, I count my bless-ings in-stead of sheep. And I fall a-

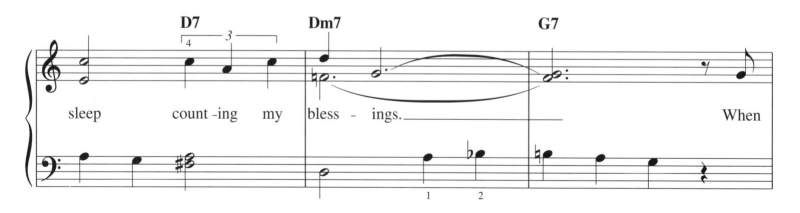

sleep count-ing my bless-ings. When

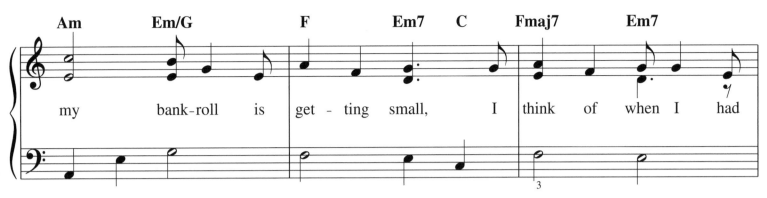

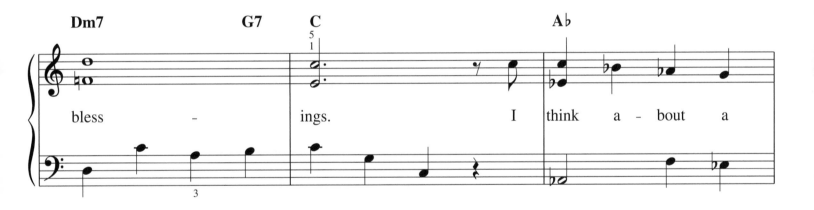

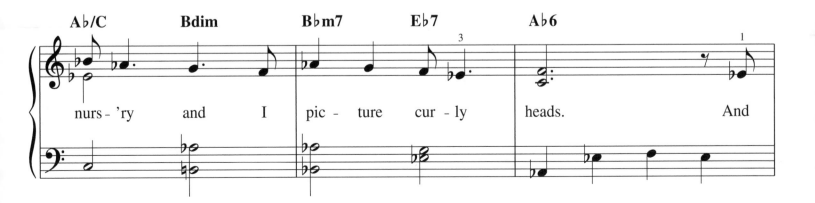

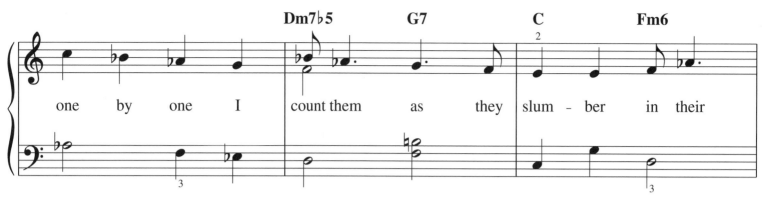

one by one I count them as they slum - ber in their

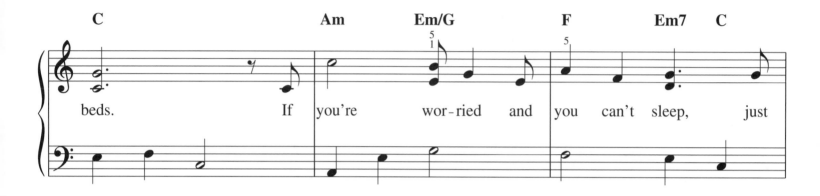

beds. If you're wor-ried and you can't sleep, just

count your bless-ings in-stead of sheep. And you'll fall a-sleep count-ing your

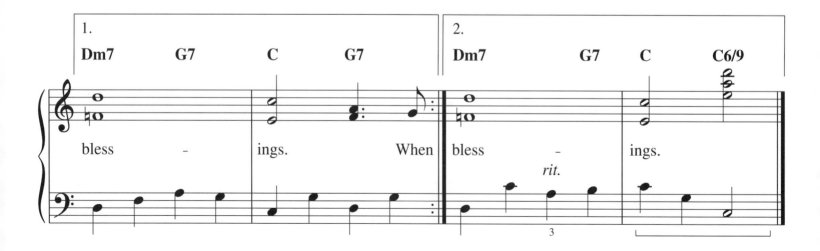

1.

bless - ings. When

2.

bless - ings.

GOD BLESS AMERICA

Words and Music by
IRVING BERLIN

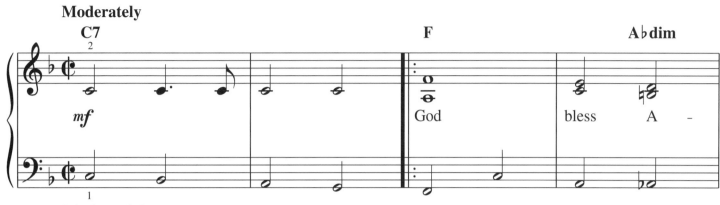

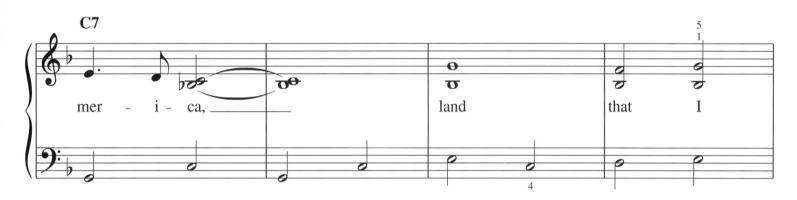

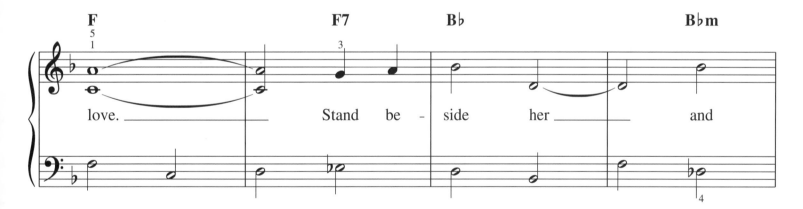

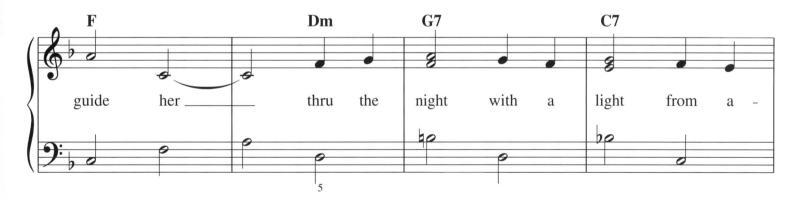

20

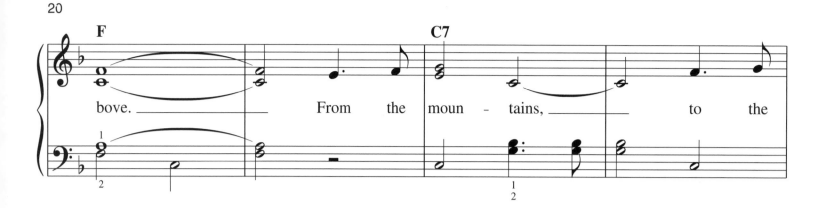

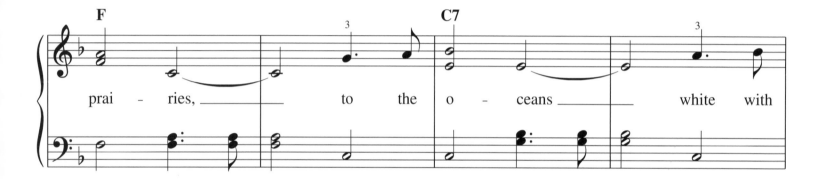

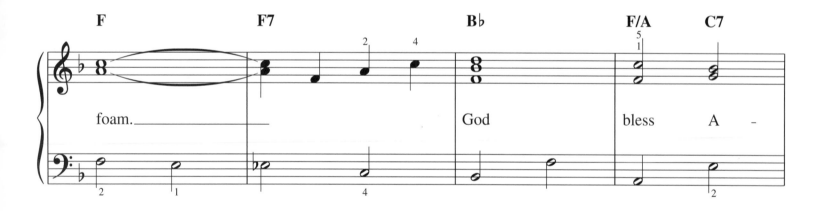

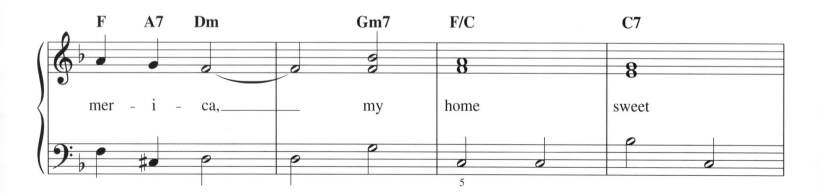

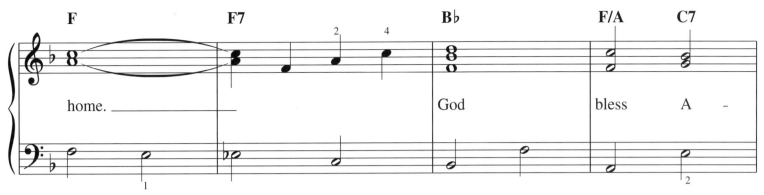

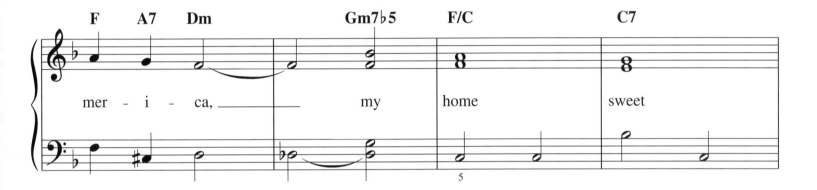

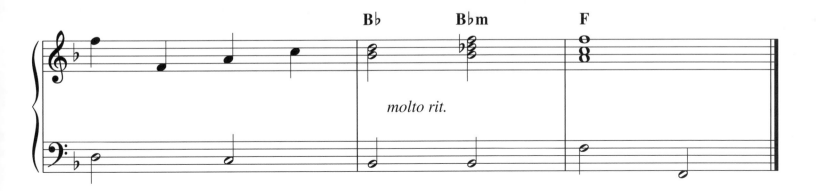

FROM A DISTANCE

Words and Music by
JULIE GOLD

With pedal

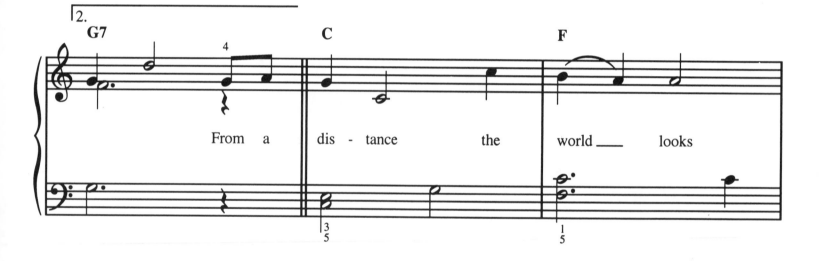

From a dis - tance the world ____ looks

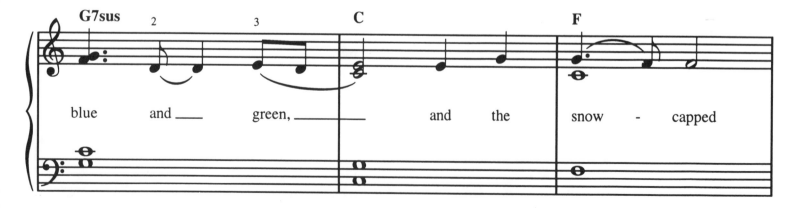

blue and ____ green, ____ and the snow - capped

23

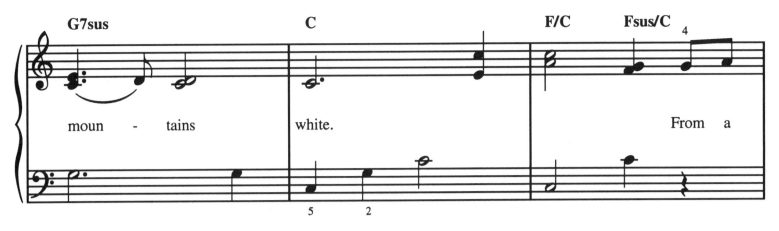

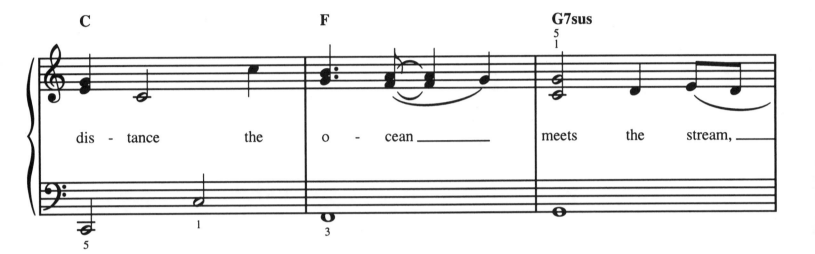

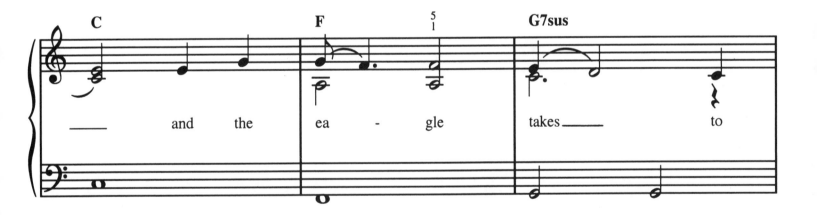

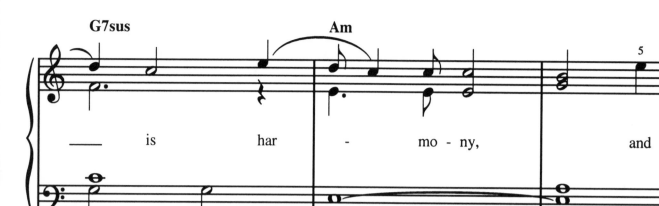

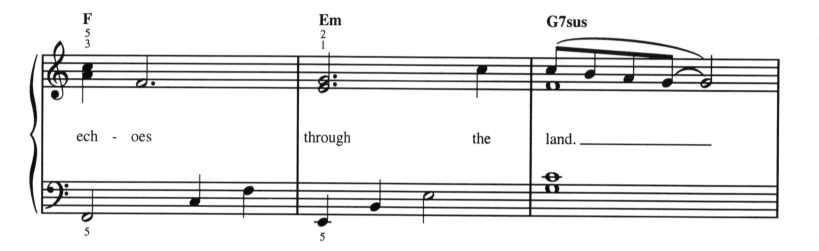

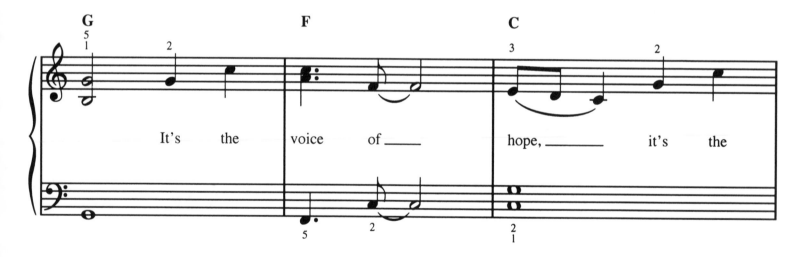

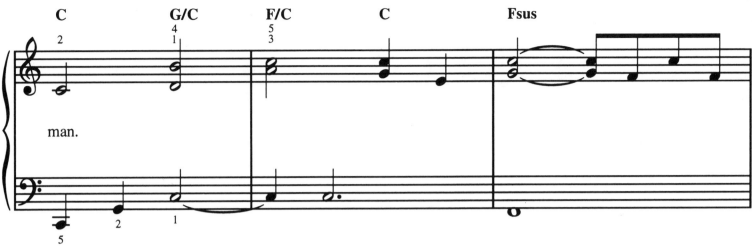

man.

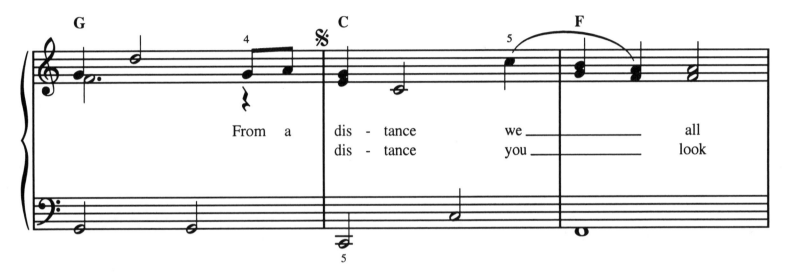

From a dis - tance we _____ all
dis - tance you _____ look

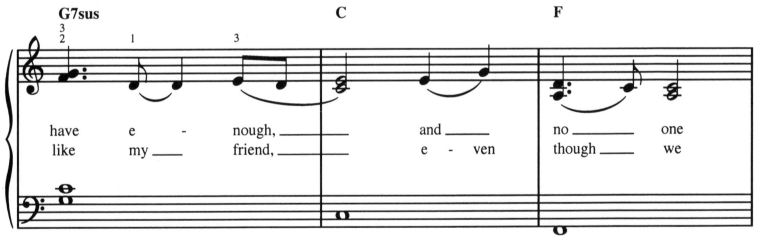

have e - nough, _____ and _____ no _____ one
like my _____ friend, _____ e - ven though _____ we

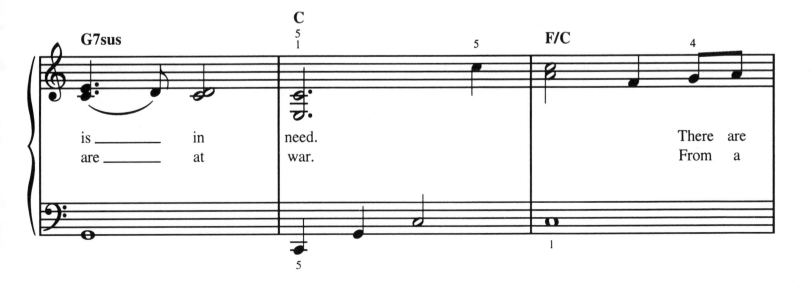

is _____ in need.
are _____ at war.

There are
From a

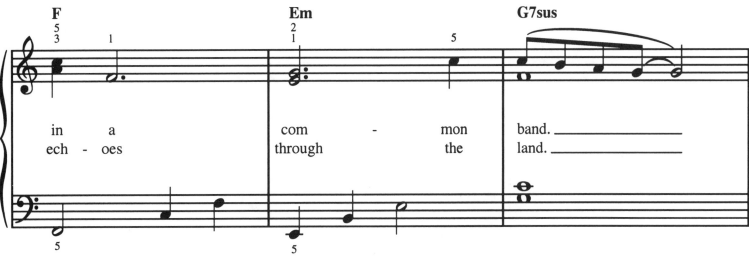

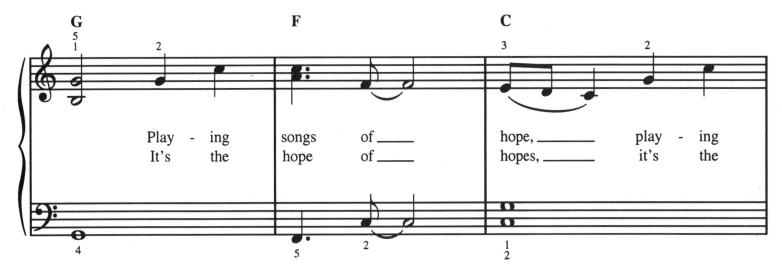

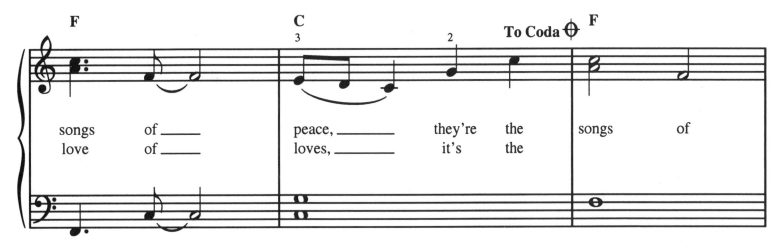

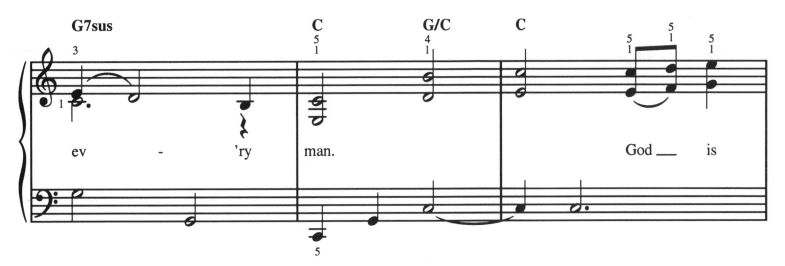

28

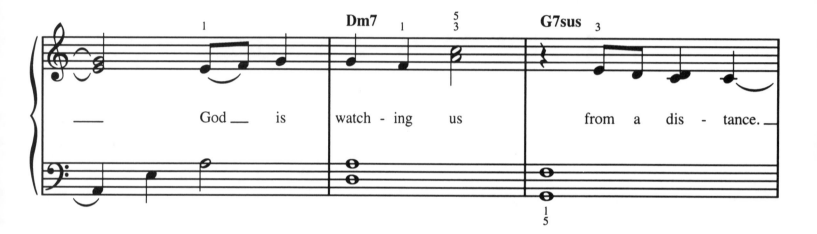

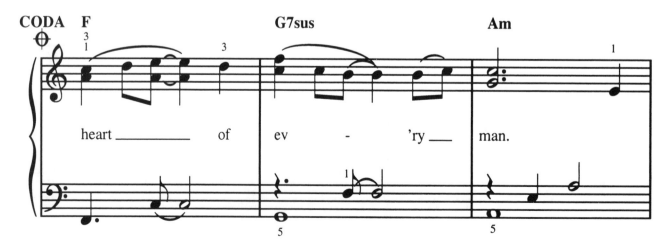

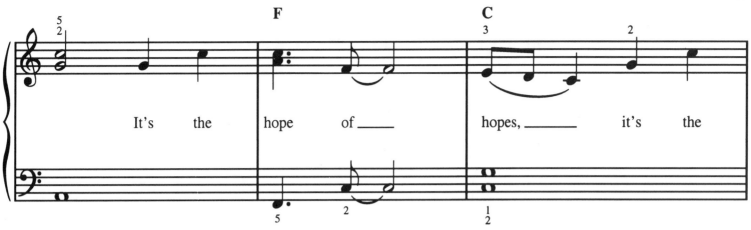

It's   the   hope   of ___   hopes, ___   it's   the

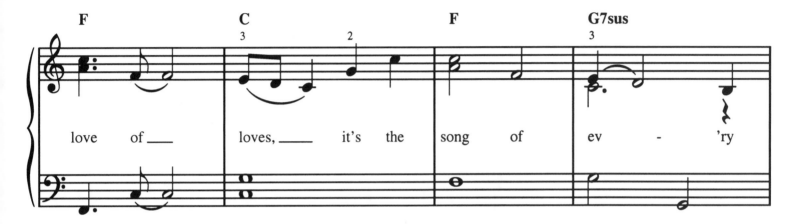

love   of ___   loves, ___   it's   the   song   of   ev -   'ry

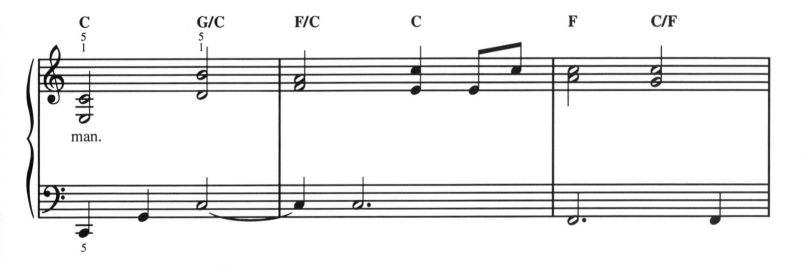

man.

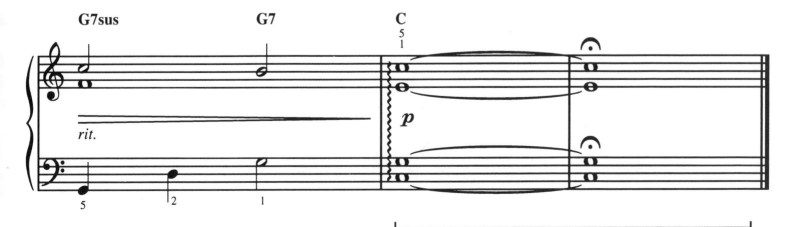

rit.   *p*

GIVE ME YOUR TIRED, YOUR POOR

from the Stage Production MISS LIBERTY

Words by EMMA LAZARUS
From the Poem "The New Colossus"
Music by IRVING BERLIN

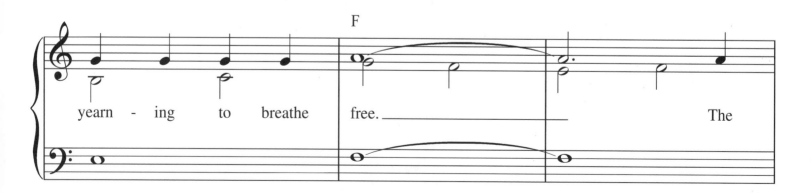

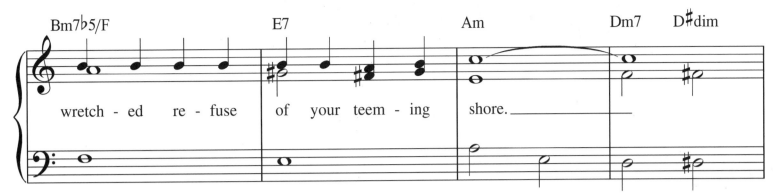

Bm7♭5/F — E7 — Am — Dm7 — D♯dim

wretch - ed re - fuse of your teem - ing shore.____

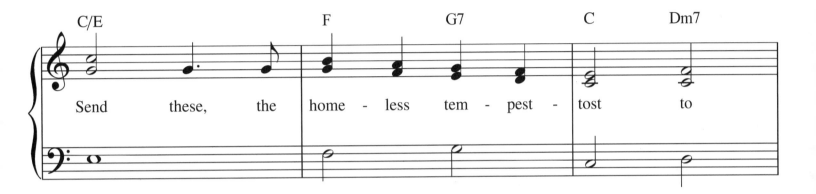

C/E — F — G7 — C — Dm7

Send these, the home - less tem - pest - tost to

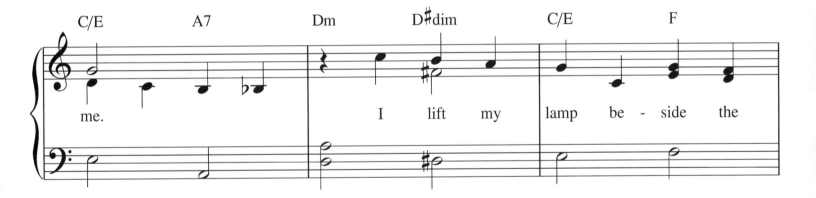

C/E — A7 — Dm — D♯dim — C/E — F

me. I lift my lamp be - side the

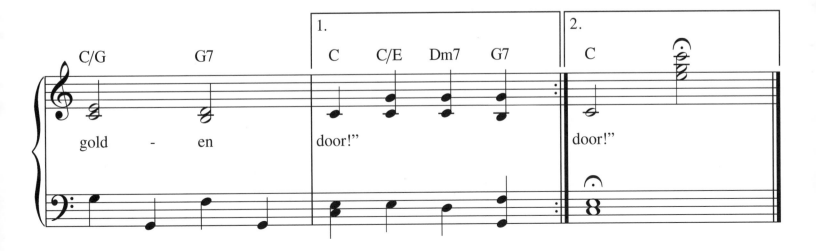

C/G — G7 — 1. C C/E Dm7 G7 — 2. C

gold - en door!" door!"

GOD OF OUR FATHERS

Words by DANIEL CRANE ROBERTS
Music by GEORGE WILLIAM WARREN

Majestically

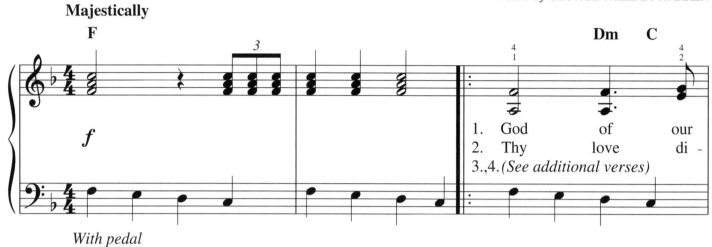

1. God of our
2. Thy love di-
3.,4. *(See additional verses)*

With pedal

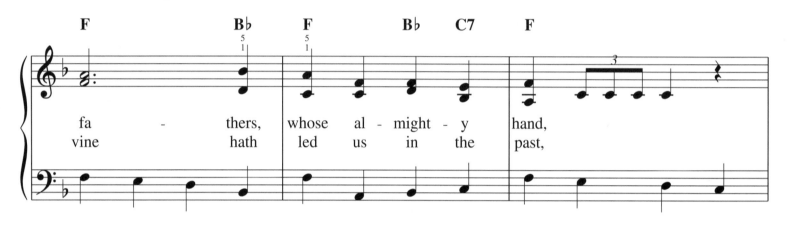

fa - thers, whose al - might - y hand,
vine, hath led us in the past,

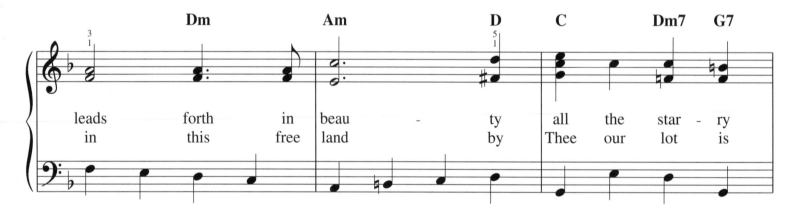

leads forth in beau - ty
in this free land by

all the star - ry
Thee our lot is

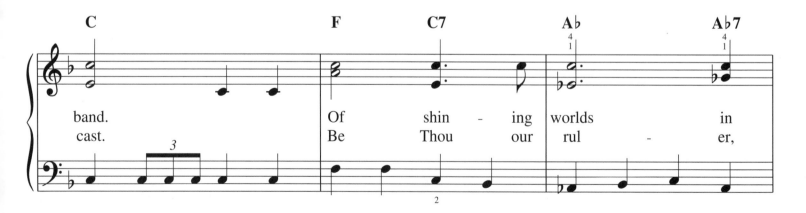

band. Of shin - ing worlds in
cast. Be Thou our rul - er,

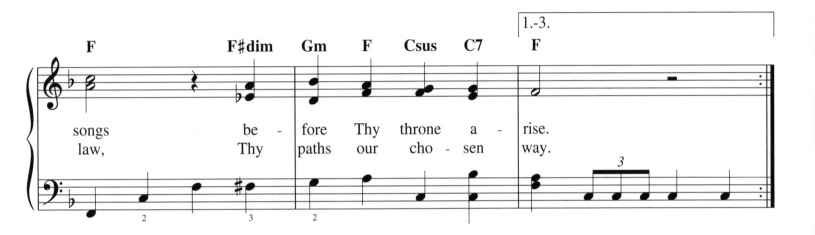

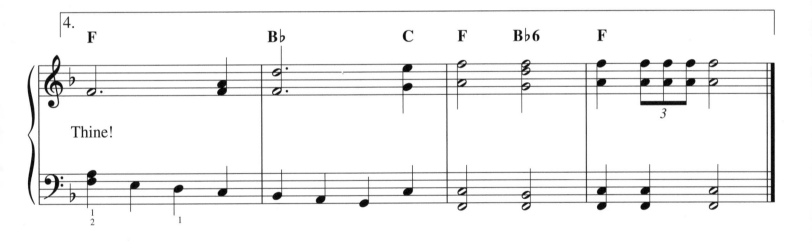

Additional Verses

3. From war's alarms, from deadly pestilence,
   Be Thy strong arm our ever sure defense.
   Thy true religion in our hearts increase,
   Thy bounteous goodness nourish us in peace.

4. Refresh Thy people on their toilsome way,
   Lead us from night to never ending day.
   Fill all our lives with love and grace divine,
   And glory, laud, and praise be ever Thine! Amen.

I BELIEVE

Words and Music by ERVIN DRAKE, IRVIN GRAHAM,
JIMMY SHIRL and AL STILLMAN

Moderately, with much expression

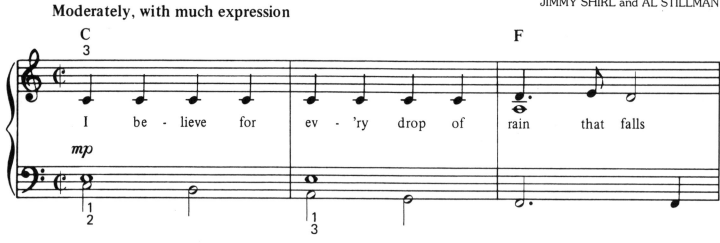

I be - lieve for ev - 'ry drop of rain that falls

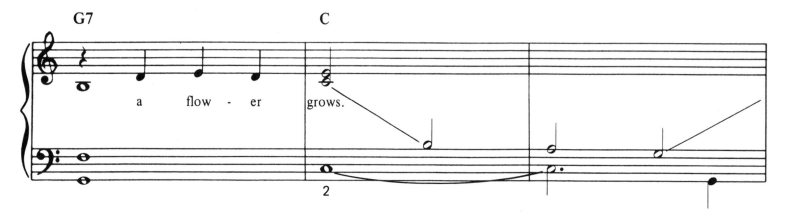

a flow - er grows.

I be - lieve that some - where in the dark - est night

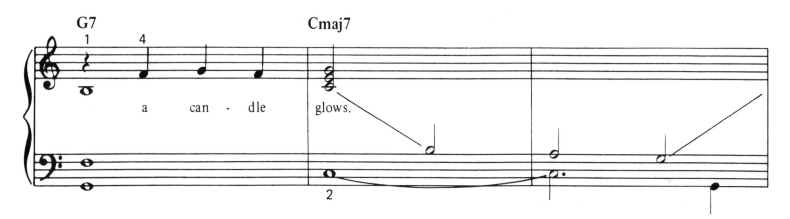

a can - dle glows.

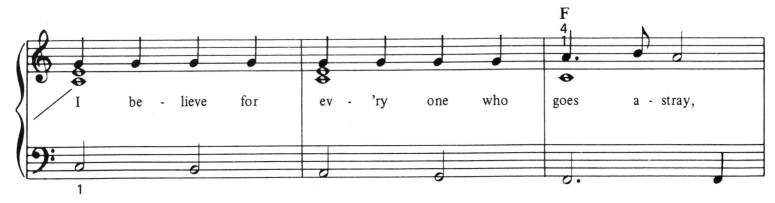

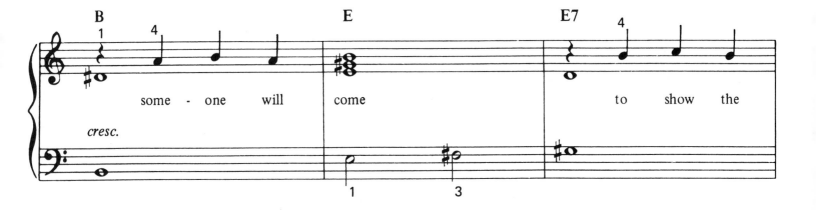

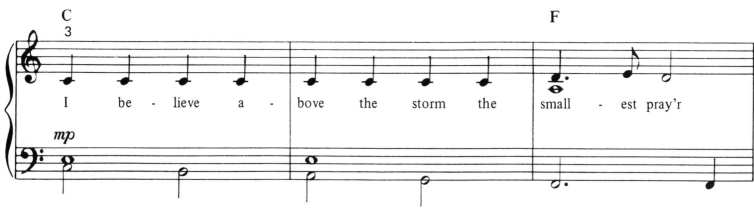

C   F

I be-lieve a-bove the storm the small-est pray'r

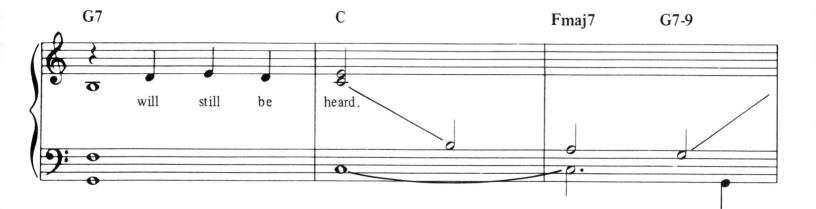

G7   C   Fmaj7   G7-9

will still be heard.

C   F

I be-lieve that some-one in the great some-where

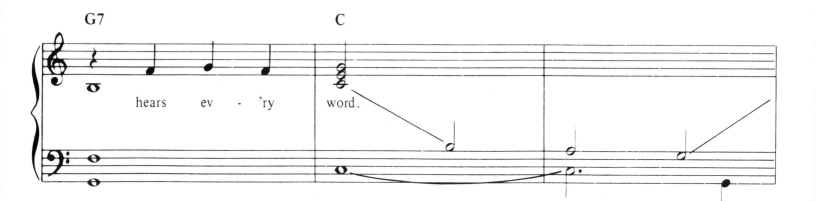

G7   C

hears ev-'ry word.

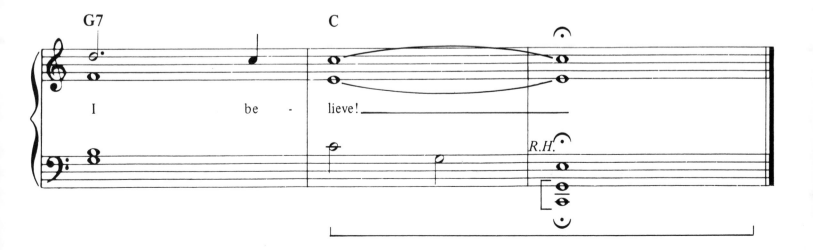

IF I HAD A HAMMER

(The Hammer Song)

Words and Music by LEE HAYS
and PETE SEEGER

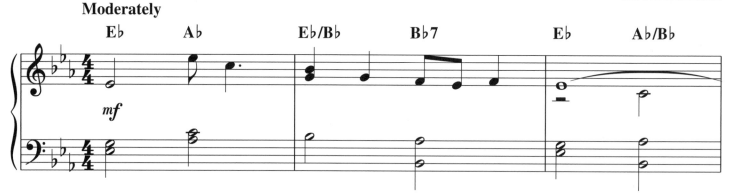

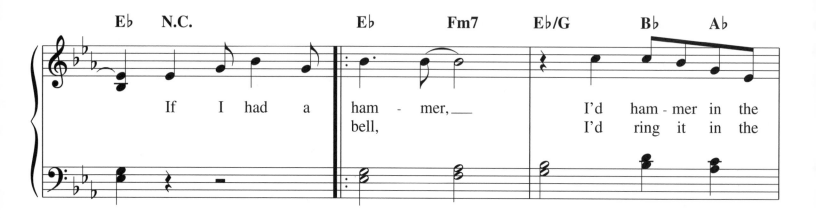

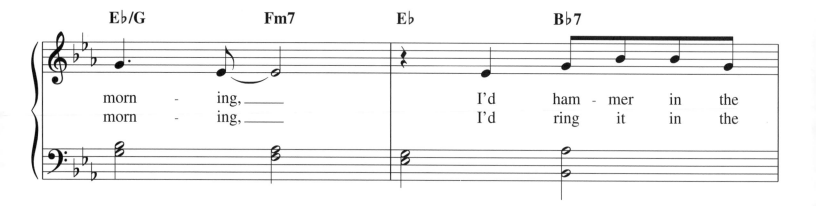

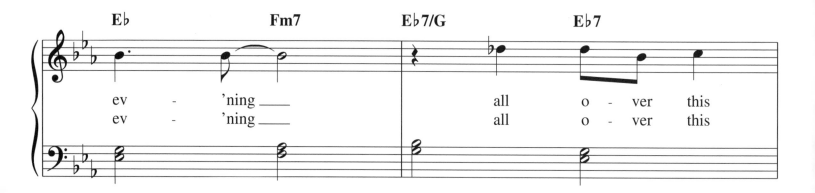

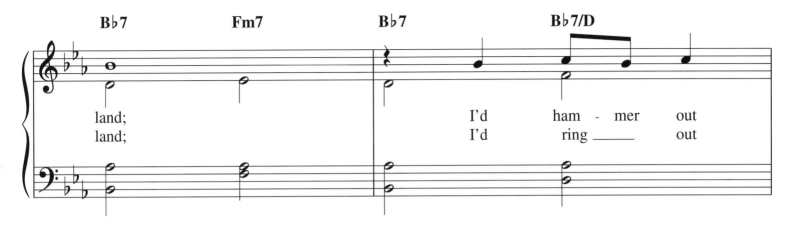

land;
land;

I'd hammer out
I'd ring ____ out

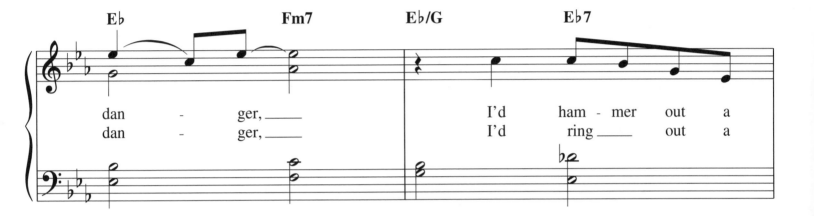

dan - ger, ____
dan - ger, ____

I'd hammer out a
I'd ring ____ out a

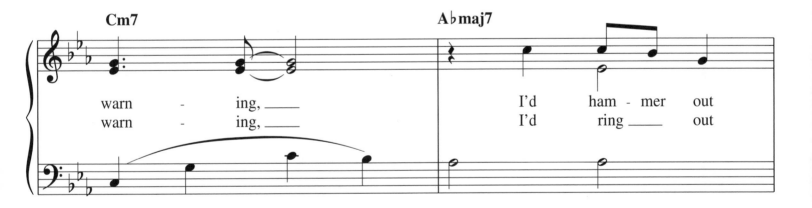

warn - ing, ____
warn - ing, ____

I'd hammer out
I'd ring ____ out

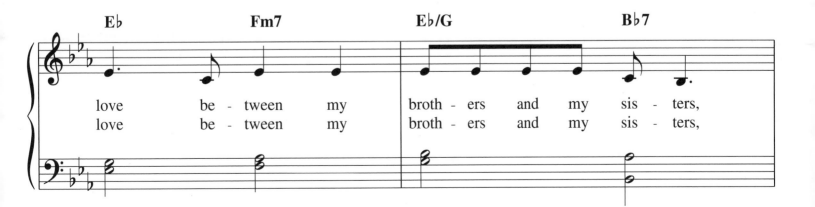

love be - tween my
love be - tween my

broth - ers and my sis - ters,
broth - ers and my sis - ters,

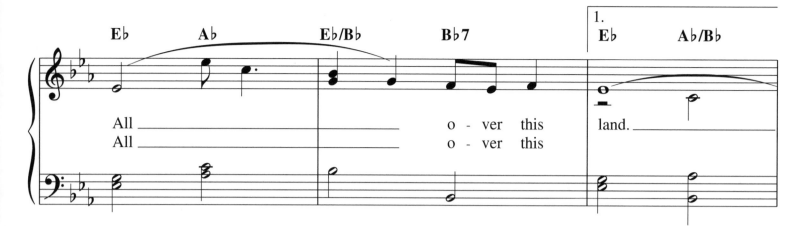

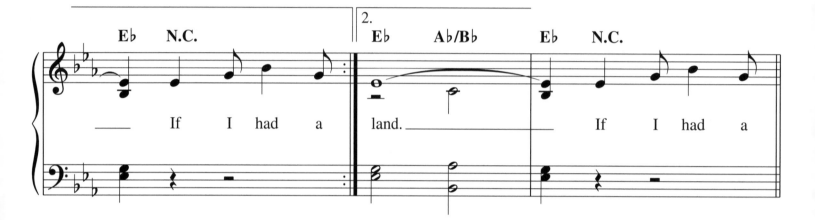

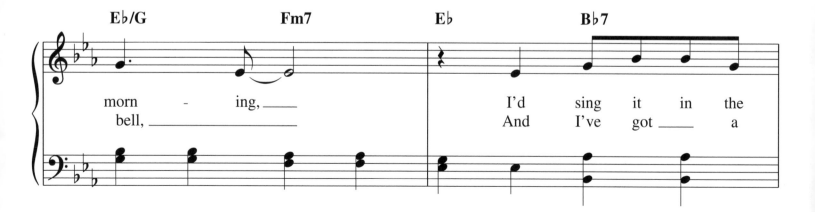

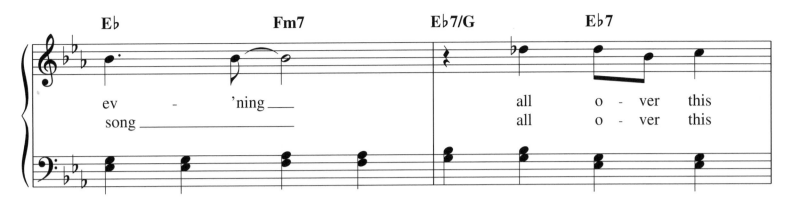

ev - 'ning ___
song _____

all o - ver this
all o - ver this

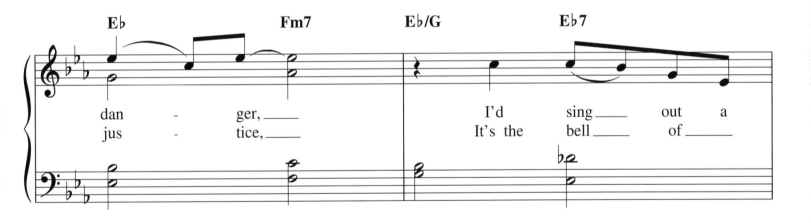

land;
land;

I'd sing ___ out
It's the ham - mer of

dan - ger, ___
jus - tice, ___

I'd sing ___ out a
It's the bell ___ of ___

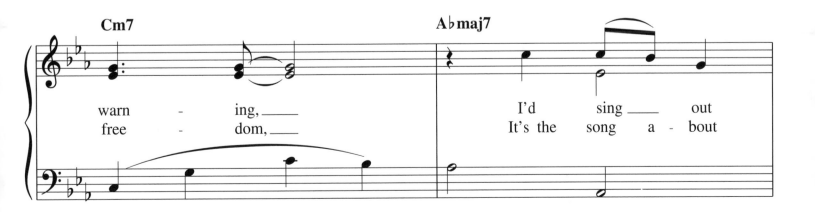

warn - ing, ___
free - dom, ___

I'd sing ___ out
It's the song a - bout

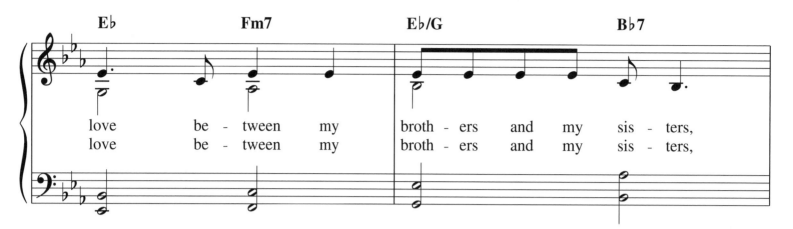

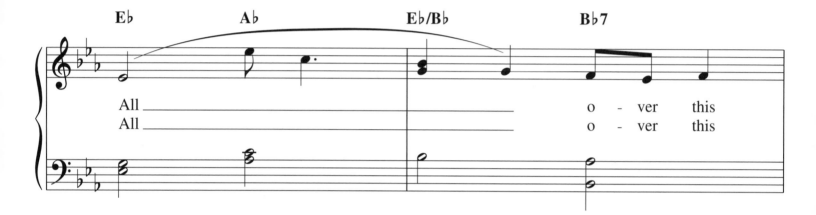

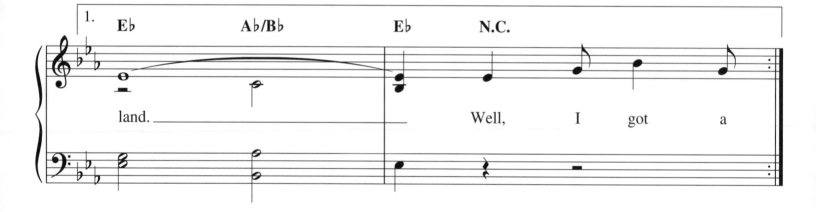

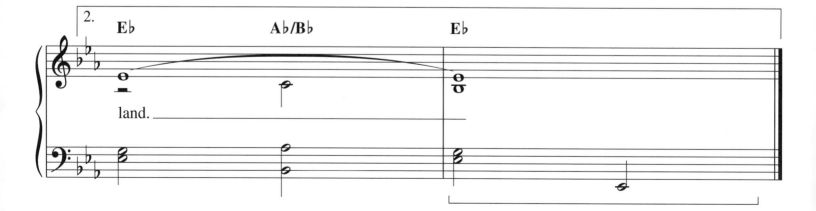

MY COUNTRY, 'TIS OF THEE
(America)

Words by SAMUEL FRANCIS SMITH
Music from *Thesaurus Musicus*

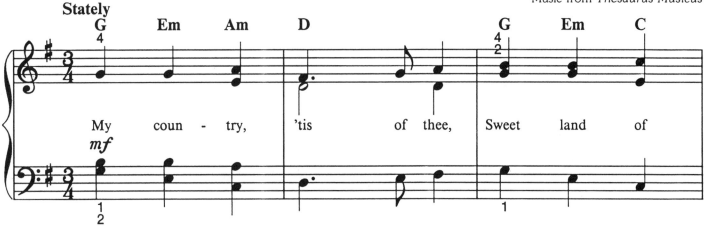

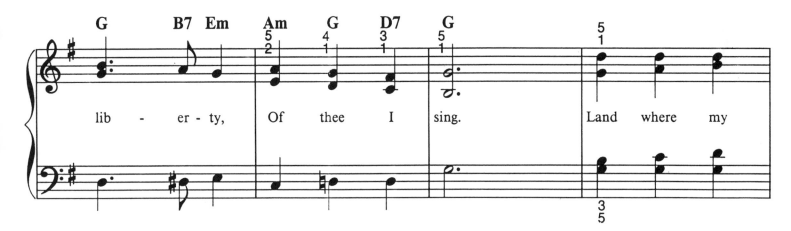

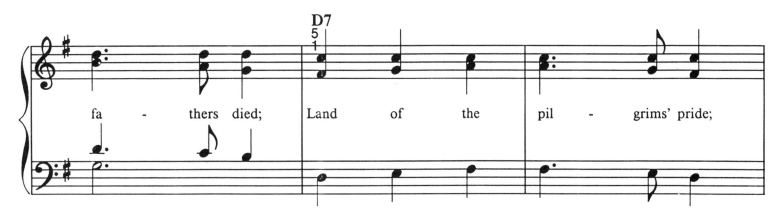

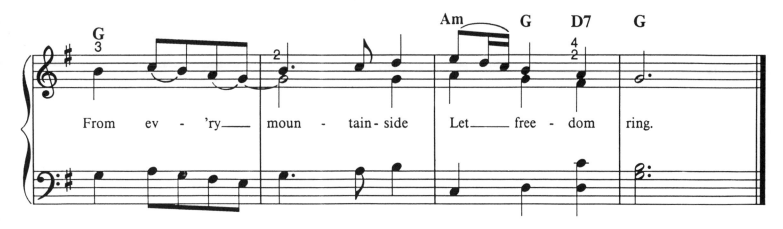

O GOD, OUR HELP IN AGES PAST

Words by ISAAC WATTS
Music by WILLIAM CROFT

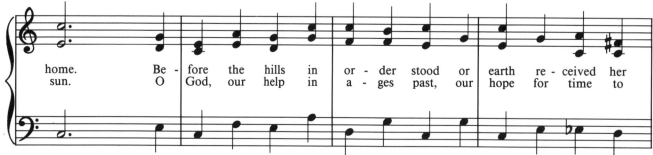

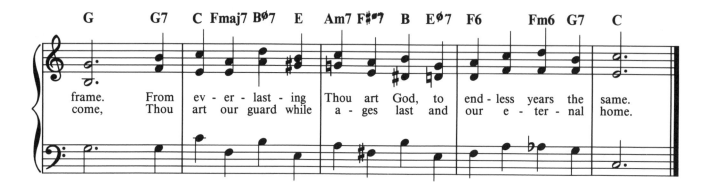

THE STAR SPANGLED BANNER

Words by FRANCIS SCOTT KEY
Music by JOHN STAFFORD SMITH

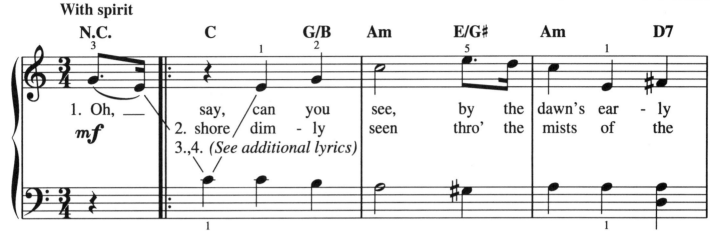

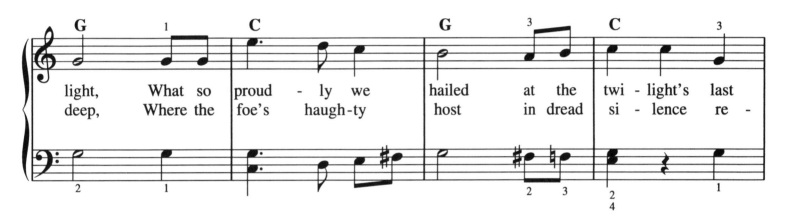

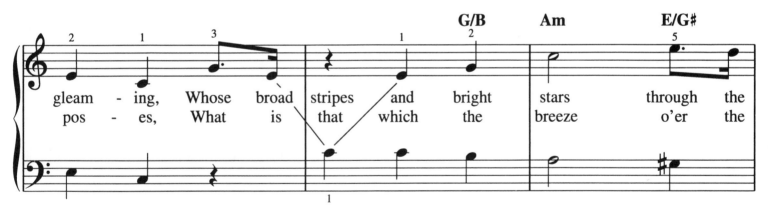

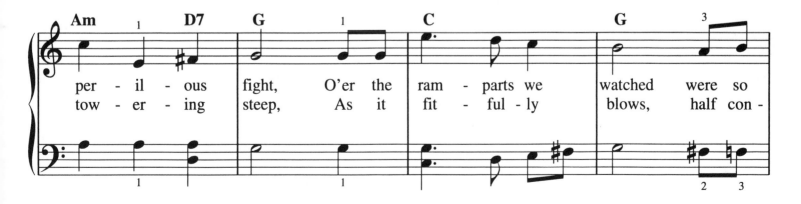

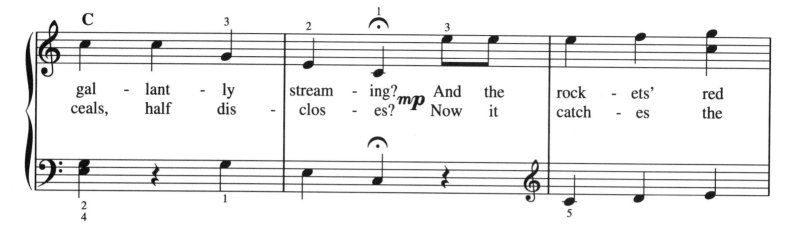

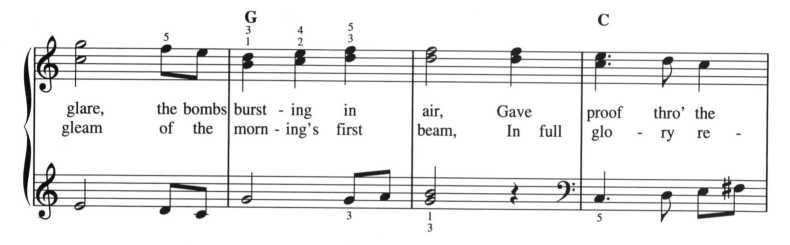

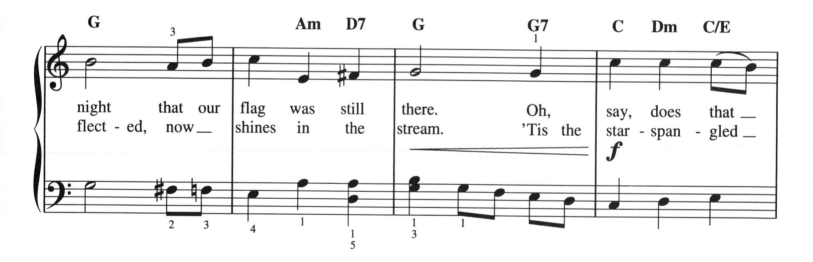

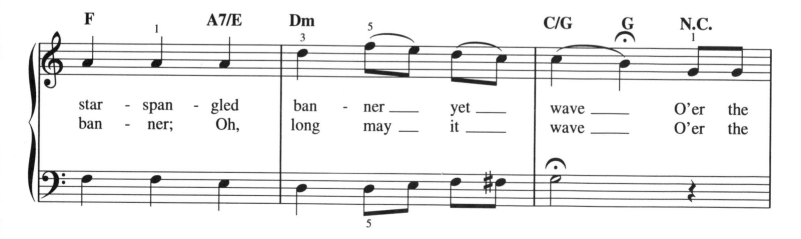

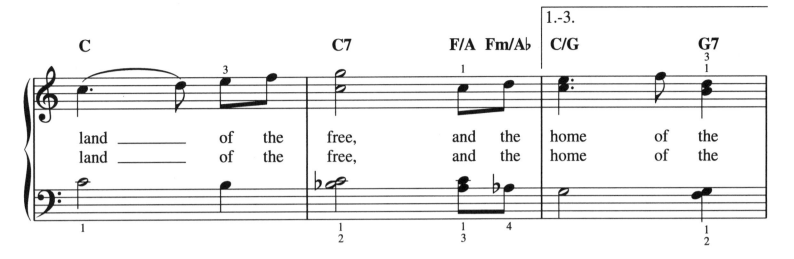

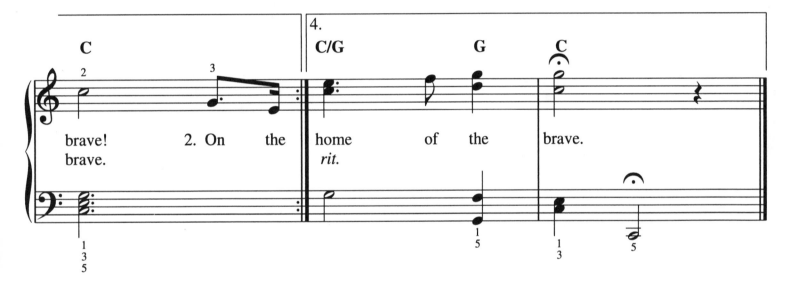

Additional Lyrics

3. And where is the band who so vauntingly swore,
   That the havoc of war and the battle's confusion
   A home and a country they'd leave us no more?
   Their blood has wash'd out their foul footstep's pollution.
   No refuge could save the hireling and slave
   From the terror of flight, or the gloom of the grave:
   And the star-spangled banner in triumph doth wave
   O'er the land of the free, and the home of the brave!

4. Oh, thus be it ever, when freemen shall stand
   Between their loved homes and the war's desolation;
   Blest with victory and peace, may the heaven-rescued land
   Praise the power that hath made and preserved us a nation!
   Then conquer we must, when our cause it is just,
   And this be our motto: "In God is our trust!"
   And the star-spangled banner in triumph shall wave,
   O'er the land of the free, and the home of the brave!

STARS AND STRIPES FOREVER

By JOHN PHILIP SOUSA

Steady march

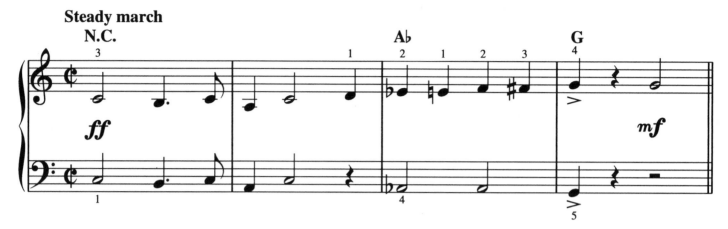

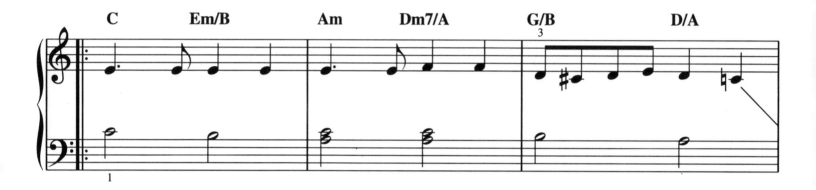

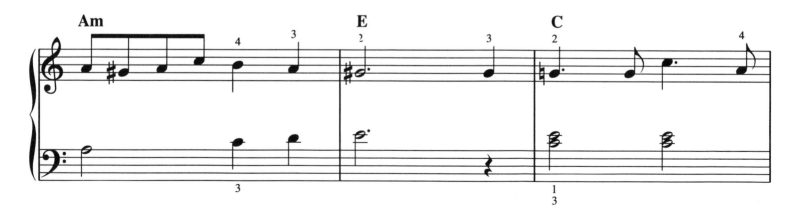

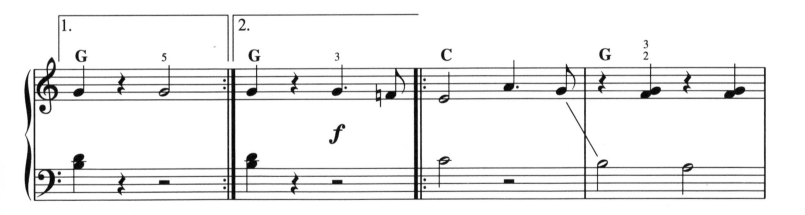

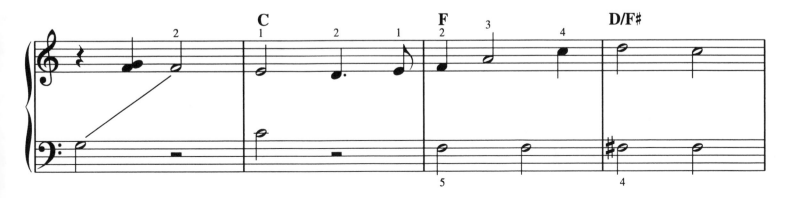

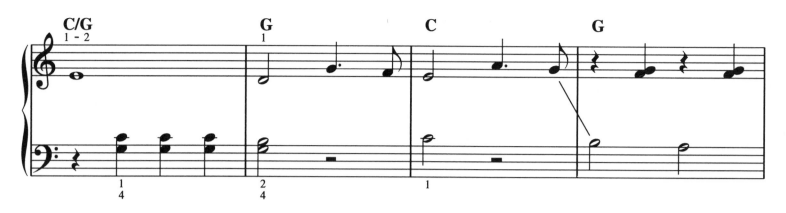

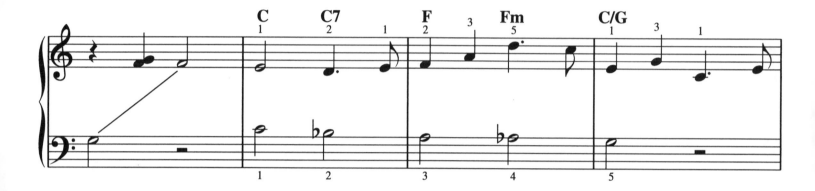

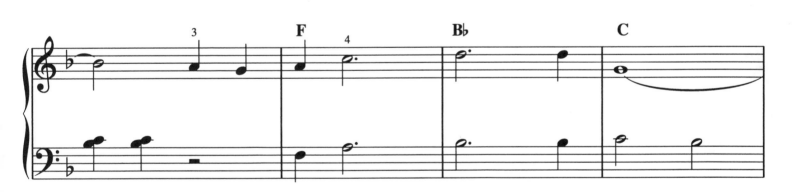

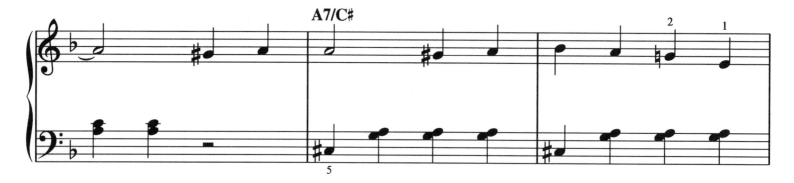

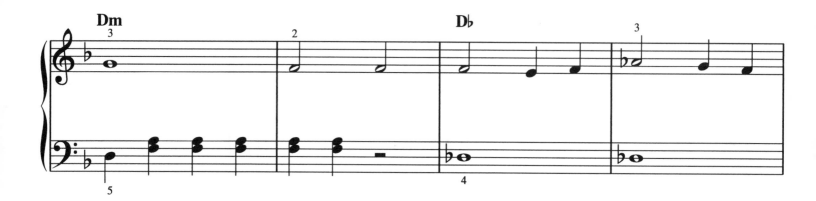

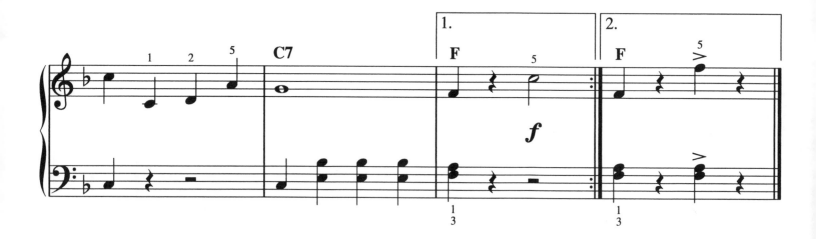

UNITED WE STAND

Words and Music by ANTHONY TOBY HILLER
and JOHN GOODISON

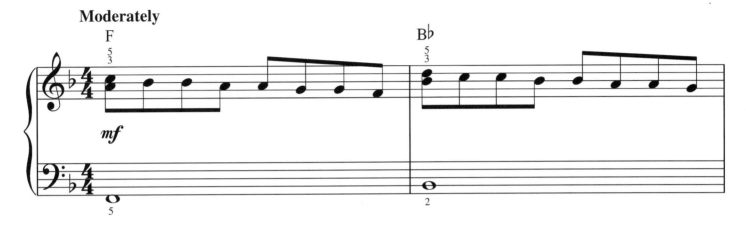

There's

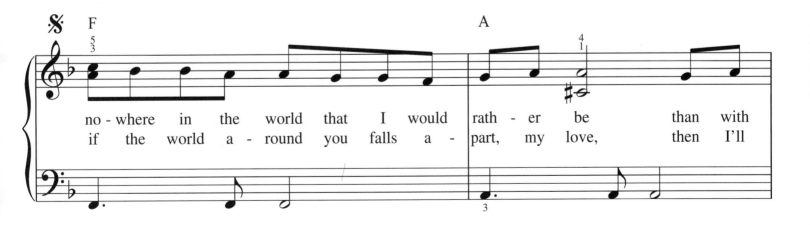

no - where in the world that I would rath - er be than with
if the world a - round you falls a - part, my love, then I'll

54

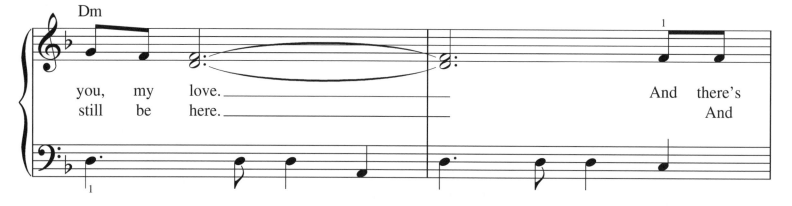

you, my love. _____ And there's
still be here. _____ And

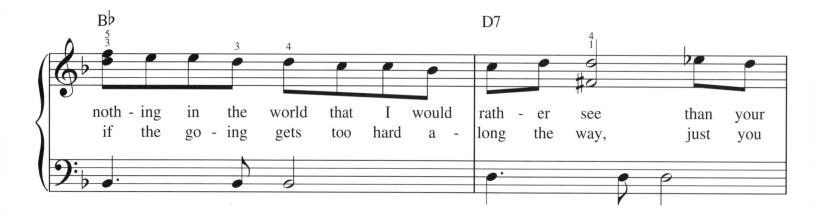

noth - ing in the world that I would rath - er see than your
if the go - ing gets too hard a - long the way, than just you

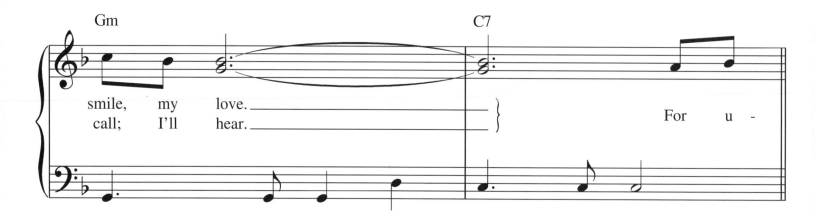

smile, my love. _____ For u -
call; I'll hear. _____

nit - ed we stand, ___ di - vid - ed we fall. ___

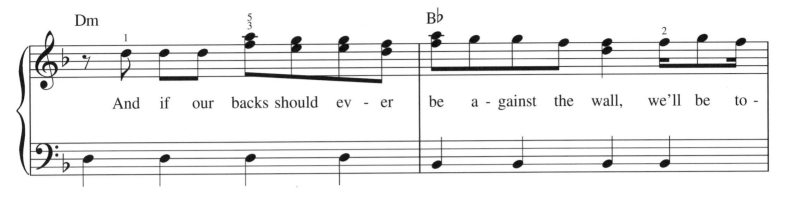

And if our backs should ev - er be a - gainst the wall, we'll be to -

geth - er, _____ to - geth - er, you and

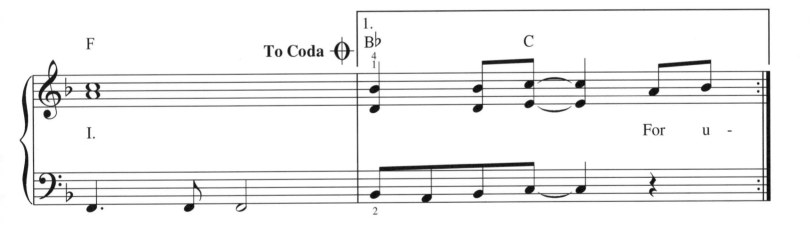

I. For u -

And

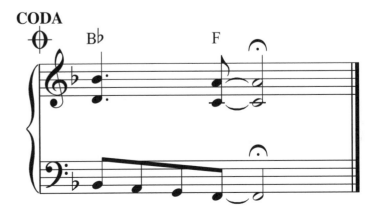

THIS IS MY COUNTRY

Words by DON RAYE
Music by AL JACOBS

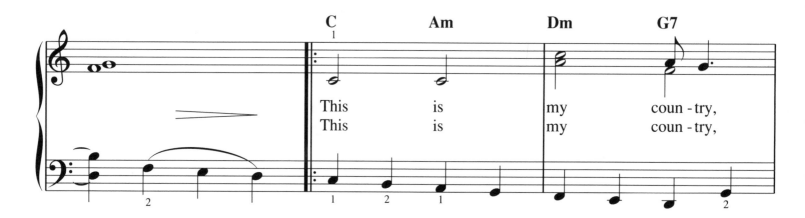

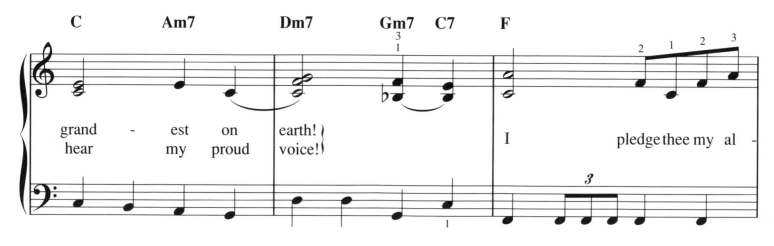

57

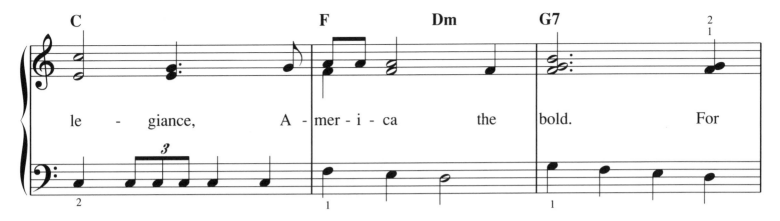

le - giance, A - mer - i - ca the bold. For

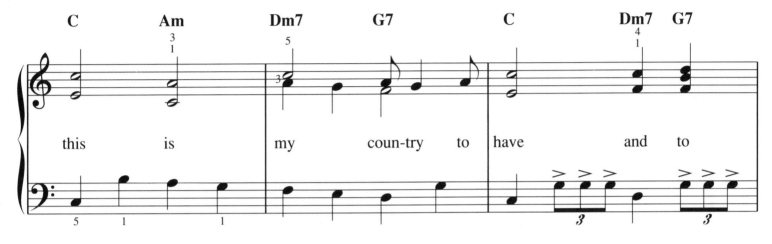

this is my coun-try to have and to

hold! hold!

THIS LAND IS YOUR LAND

Words and Music by
WOODY GUTHRIE

With gusto

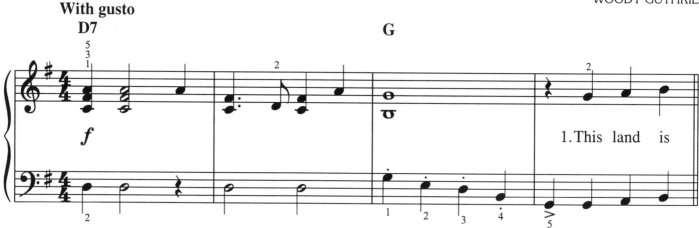

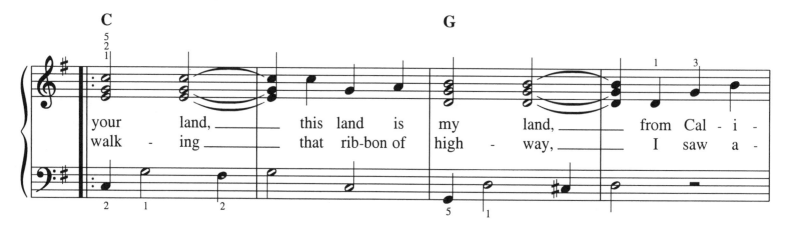

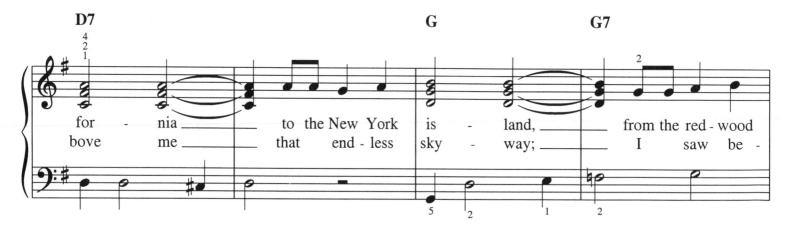

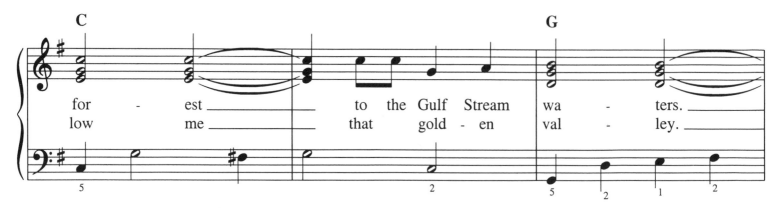

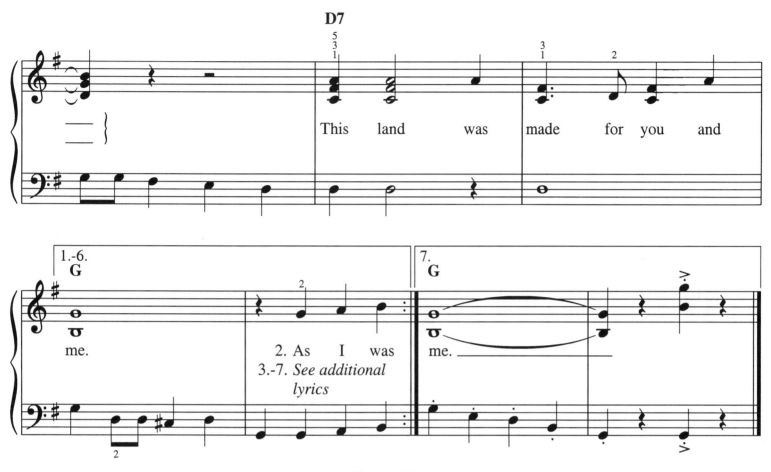

This land was made for you and

me.

2. As I was

3.-7. *See additional lyrics*

me.

Additional Lyrics

3. I've roamed and rambled and I followed my footsteps
   To the sparkling sands of her diamond deserts,
   And all around me a voice was sounding,
   "This land was made for you and me."

4. When the sun came shining, and I was strolling,
   And the wheat fields waving and the dust clouds rolling,
   As the fog was lifting, a voice was chanting,
   "This land was made for you and me."

5. As I went walking, I saw a sign there,
   And on the sign, it said "No Trespassing."
   But on the other side it didn't say nothing.
   That side was made for you and me.

6. In the shadow of the steeple I saw my people,
   By the relief office I seen my people.
   As they stood there hungry, I stood there asking,
   "Is this land made for you and me?"

7. Nobody living can ever stop me
   As I go walking that freedom highway;
   Nobody living can ever make me turn back.
   This land was made for you and me.

WE SHALL OVERCOME

Musical and Lyrical Adaptation by ZILPHIA HORTON,
FRANK HAMILTON, GUY CARAWAN and PETE SEEGER
Inspired by African American Gospel Singing,
members of the Food and Tobacco Workers Union, Charleston, SC,
and the southern Civil Rights Movement

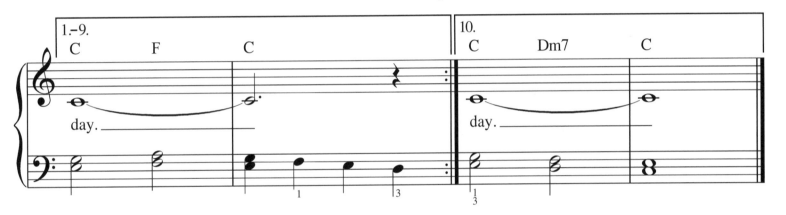

Additional Lyrics

3. We are not afraid, we are not afraid,
   We are not afraid today.
   Oh, deep in my heart I do believe
   We shall overcome some day.

4. We shall stand together, we shall stand together,
   We shall stand together - now.
   Oh, deep in my heart I do believe
   We shall overcome some day.

5. The truth will make us free,
      the truth will make us free,
   The truth will make us free some day.
   Oh, deep in my heart I do believe
   We shall overcome some day.

6. The Lord will see us through, the Lord will see us through,
   The Lord will see us through some day.
   Oh, deep in my heart I do believe
   We shall overcome some day.

7. We shall be like Him, we shall be like Him,
   We shall be like Him some day.
   Oh, deep in my heart I do believe
   We shall overcome some day.

8. We shall live in peace, we shall live in peace,
   We shall live in peace some day.
   Oh, deep in my heart I do believe
   We shall overcome some day.

9. The whole wide world around,
      the whole wide world around,
   The whole wide world around some day.
   Oh, deep in my heart I do believe
   We shall overcome some day.

10. We shall overcome, we shall overcome,
    We shall overcome some day.
    Oh, deep in my heart I do believe
    We shall overcome some day.

YOU'RE A GRAND OLD FLAG
from GEORGE M!

Words and Music by
GEORGE M. COHAN

Brightly

mf You're a grand old flag! You're a high-fly-ing flag, and for-

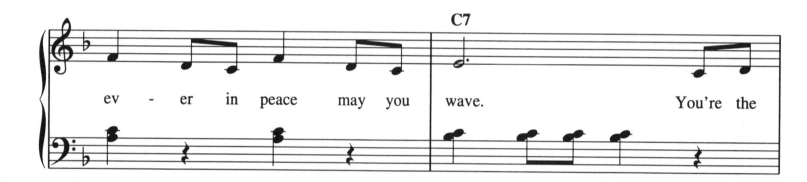

ev - er in peace may you wave. You're the

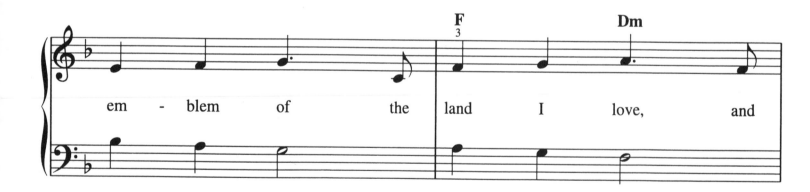

em - blem of the land I love, and

home of the free and the brave. Ev - 'ry

heart beats true un - der red, white and blue, where there's

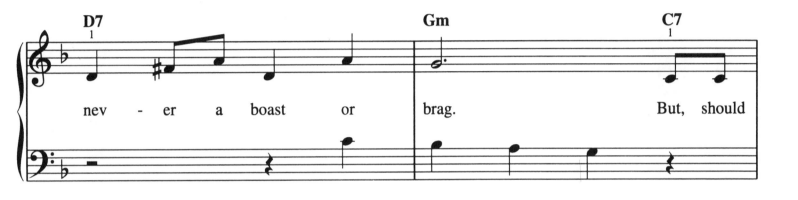

nev - er a boast or brag. But, should

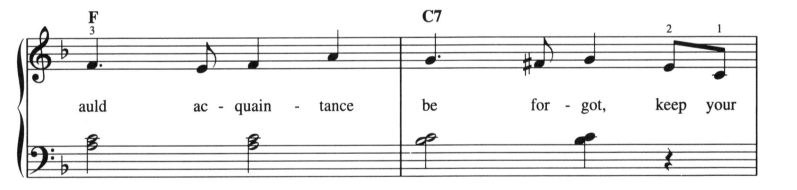

auld ac - quain - tance be for - got, keep your

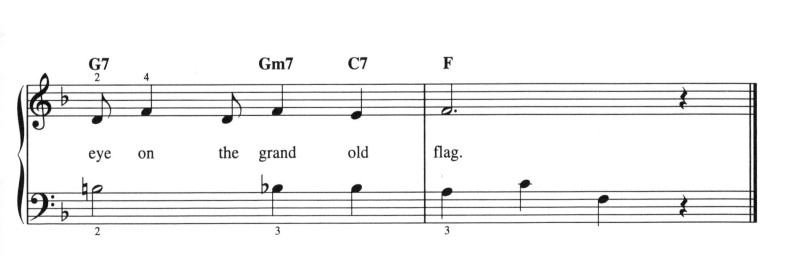

eye on the grand old flag.

It's Easy to Play Your Favorite Songs with Hal Leonard Easy Piano Books

The Best of Today's Movie Hits
16 contemporary film favorites: Change the World • Colors of the Wind • I Believe in You and Me • I Finally Found Someone • If I Had Words • Mission: Impossible Theme • When I Fall in Love • You Must Love Me • more.
00310248 ....$9.95

Playing the Blues
Over 30 great blues tunes arranged for easy piano: Baby, Won't You Please Come Home • Chicago Blues • Fine and Mellow • Heartbreak Hotel • Pinetop's Blues • St. Louis Blues • The Thrill Is Gone • more.
00310102...$12.95

The Best Songs Ever
Over 70 all-time favorite songs, featuring: All I Ask of You • Body and Soul • Call Me Irresponsible • Crazy • Edelweiss • Fly Me to the Moon • The Girl From Ipanema • Here's That Rainy Day • Imagine • Let It Be • Longer • Moon River • Moonlight in Vermont • People • Satin Doll • Save the Best for Last • Somewhere Out There • Stormy Weather • Strangers in the Night • Tears in Heaven • Unchained Melody • Unforgettable • The Way We Were • What a Wonderful World • When I Fall in Love • and more
00359223 ....$19.95

Country Love Songs
34 classic and contemporary country favorites, including: The Dance • A Few Good Things Remain • Forever and Ever Amen • I Never Knew Love • Love Can Build a Bridge • Love Without End, Amen • She Believes in Me • She Is His Only Need • Where've You Been • and more.
00110030 ....$12.95

R&B Love Songs
27 songs, including: Ain't Nothing Like the Real Thing • Easy • Exhale (Shoop Shoop) • The First Time Ever I Saw Your Face • Here and Now • I'm Your Baby Tonight • My Girl • Never Can Say Goodbye • Ooo Baby Baby • Save the Best for Last • Someday • Still • and more.
00310181 ....$12.95

Rock N Roll for Easy Piano
40 rock favorites for the piano, including: All Shook Up • At the Hop • Chantilly Lace • Great Balls of Fire • Lady Madonna • The Shoop Shoop Song (It's in His Kiss) • The Twist • Wooly Bully • and more.
00222544..$12.95

I'll Be Seeing You
50 Songs of World War II
A salute to the music and memories of WWII, including a chronology of events on the homefront, dozens of photos, and 50 radio favorites of the GIs and their families back home. Includes: Boogie Woogie Bugle Boy • Don't Sit Under the Apple Tree (With Anyone Else But Me) • I Don't Want to Walk Without You • Moonlight in Vermont • and more.
00310147..$18.95

The Really Big Book of Children's Songs
63 kids' hits: Alley Cat Song • Any Dream Will Do • Circle of Life • The Grouch Song • Hakuna Matata • I Won't Grow Up • Kum-Ba-Yah • Monster Mash • My Favorite Things • Sesame Street Theme • Winnie the Pooh • You've Got a Friend in Me • and more.
00310372...$15.95

Broadway Jazz Standards
34 super songs from the stage: All the Things You Are • Bewitched • Come Rain or Come Shine • I Could Write a Book • Just in Time • The Lady Is a Tramp • Mood Indigo • My Funny Valentine • Old Devil Moon • Satin Doll • Small World • and more.
00310428...$11.95

Best of Cole Porter
Over 30 songs, including: Be a Clown • Begin the Beguine • Easy to Love • From This Moment On • In the Still of the Night • Night and Day • So in Love • Too Darn Hot • You Do Something to Me • You'd Be So Nice to Come Home To • and more
00311576...$14.95